For some Christians, trapped in [...] *are too afraid to question the shib[...]* *evangelicalism, reading this thought[...]* *experience, akin perhaps to an Ho[...] [...] [...] The author encourages evangelical Christians to think "outside the box", but in the process he is not undermining faith but building up faith. This is a book written not just by a gifted journalist, but also by an experienced pastor who is concerned to help evangelical Christians relate their faith to the world as it really is. Written for Christians who want to love the Lord their God with their minds as well as their hearts, this is a lively and thought-provoking book which I warmly commend – not just to individual readers, but also to church home-groups prepared to study and discuss together.*

Paul Beasley-Murray, chairman of Ministry Today and a former principal of Spurgeon's College

Incisive, warm, articulate – this book is a breath of fresh air. Buy it, read it and… breathe.

Jeff Lucas, broadcaster, speaker, and author

Mark Woods uses his journalistic skills and his pastor's heart to raise questions about what are considered to be settled issues in Christian theology and practices. Does God have a plan for our lives and what is the purpose of evangelism? Do we really believe in eternal punishment and why do we need the church? What is the purpose of prayer and what is the nature of preaching? He doesn't just raise questions, he leads us through a reexamination of our own thinking. It is an exciting, challenging, and highly readable work.

Dr Mitch Carnell, author and communications expert

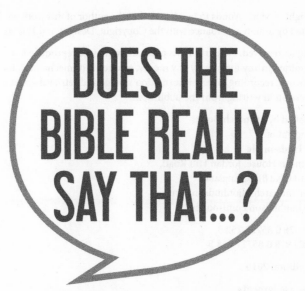

DOES THE BIBLE REALLY SAY THAT...?

Challenging our assumptions
in the light of Scripture

Mark Woods

MONARCH
BOOKS

Oxford, UK, & Grand Rapids, Michigan, USA

Published by Monarch Books
an imprint of
Lion Hudson plc
Wilkinson House, Jordan Hill Road,
Oxford OX2 8DR, England
Email: monarch@lionhudson.com
www.lionhudson.com/monarch

ISBN 978 0 85721 752 3
e-ISBN 978 0 85721 758 5

First edition 2016

Acknowledgments
Scripture quotations marked "NIV" are taken from The Holy Bible, New International Version Anglicised. Copyright © 1979, 1984, 2011 Biblica, formerly International Bible Society. All rights reserved. Anglicised edition first published in Great Britain 1979 by Hodder & Stoughton, a Hachette UK company.
Scripture quotations marked "ESV" are taken from The Holy Bible, English Standard Version® (ESV®) Copyright © 2001 by Crossway, a publishing ministry of Good News Publishers. All rights reserved. ESV Text Edition: 2011.
Scripture quotations marked "NET Bible" are taken from The NET Bible® copyright ©1996–2006 by Biblical Studies Press, L.L.C., http://netbible.com All rights reserved.
p. 16: Extract from "I Do Not Know What Lies Ahead" by Alfred B. Smith & Eugene Clark, copyright © 1958 New Spring Publishing/Imagem (Adm. Small Stone Media BV/Song Solutions www.songsolutions.org). All rights reserved. Used by permission.
pp. 90–91: Extracts from The Hiding Place by Corrie Ten Boom and John and Elizabeth Sherrill, copyright © Corrie Ten Boom and John and Elizabeth Sherrill, 1971. Used by permission.

A catalogue record for this book is available from the British Library

Printed and bound in the UK, July 2016, LH26

Dedicated with thanks to Kathy,
who helps me think more clearly and feel more strongly.

Contents

Contents

Acknowledgments

I would like to thank the two churches I have pastored for the wisdom they have shared with me. They know who they are. In both of them I learned far more than I taught.

I would also like to thank the editor of the *Baptist Ministers' Journal* for permission to draw on an article I wrote some years ago for part of chapter two. I have drawn on an interview originally published in *The Baptist Times* in part of chapter five.

Much of the thinking in these pieces was honed through my daily work for *Christian Today* (www.christiantoday.com). I appreciate the opportunity it gives me to grapple with big questions, and fast-approaching deadlines have often forced me to continue wrestling with issues when I would much rather have stopped.

And sincere thanks too to my editor at Lion Hudson, Ali Hull, for her encouragement and support.

Foreword

I started to think about this book after writing an article for the website I work for, on whether God has a plan for our lives. I was pretty clear that he doesn't – or rather not in the way people usually take that saying to mean. There are better ways of thinking about how he deals with us, ways that are truer to Scripture and to the reality of the lives we live.

But then I started wondering about whether there are other things that we either take for granted, or just don't feel we can talk about, that deserve a hard look. What about things like forgiveness, and evangelism, and spiritual growth? What about Genesis? Are we missing some of the richness and depth of our faith because we don't like to ask the questions we ought to ask? Are there different ways of thinking about old truths that might challenge and inspire us? Are there, even, old truths that turn out not to be true after all?

I have written as a Christian in the evangelical tradition. I've been a Baptist pastor and a journalist; both of these experiences have shaped me and affected the way I've approached the themes of this book. My aim is to build readers up, but also to ask the hard questions about how their faith actually works.

I've found myself challenged and sometimes baffled by the subjects I've had to address, but often blessed, as well, as I've grappled with Scripture and made connections I hadn't thought of before. I have learned as I have written, and met often with God as I've struggled to form sentences and paragraphs that make sense. I hope that, as you read this book, you'll meet him too.

I have tried to economize on footnotes and references; these will be rare, and used only where quotes and sources can't easily be located online.

1

God may not have a plan for your life, and that's OK

Around fifty years ago, in 1966, a terrible tragedy struck a Welsh valley town. It was a part of the world where death from accident or neglect, sometimes on a larger scale than we would ever tolerate today, was not uncommon: coal mines are dangerous places to work. This was different, though. A slag heap above the village of Aberfan, undermined by an underground spring, collapsed. Within a few minutes, 40,000 cubic metres of debris had flowed downhill and covered a farm, some terraced houses – and Pantglas Junior School, where the children had just left the assembly hall after morning prayers. Altogether, 116 children and twenty-eight adults died.

I'm too young to remember it, but I've seen the black-and-white footage of the aftermath: the crowds at the funeral, a long trench with its small coffins all in a line, the heaps of flowers. And there was a clergyman interviewed by a journalist. He's clearly broken by what he's seen, but he manages to choke out: "There must be a plan. I have to believe there's a plan."

That belief – that God has a plan; that everything happens for a reason; that, although we can't see it, he's shaping the events of our lives for good – has become a fundamental belief for a great many evangelical Christians. It survives disappointments, mistakes, wrong turns, and even tragedy, public or personal. God has a wonderful plan for your life.

It's something that we tend not to question, any more than we question basic doctrines like the Trinity. Somehow, whatever happens to us is God's will. There is a reason for the bad things, and ultimately it's a good reason because God is a good God. Saying you don't believe God has a plan for your life is like saying you don't believe he cares about you at all.

I understand where people who think like this are coming from. They have a deep sense of the sovereignty of God. They want to affirm his power. They read texts in the Bible that speak of his ordering events and controlling history, and they want to be faithful Bible believers. They're also dismayed by any idea that things just happen. We might not know why they happen, but God is working to his own agenda.

The Aberfan clergyman in the clip I watched just could not face believing that what had just taken place was a terrible, random catastrophe. Somehow it had to make sense, and he clung to the idea that God had a plan as a drowning man clings to a lifebelt. But here's my problem. If God has a wonderful plan for my life, he had a wonderful plan for the lives of those children too. And I don't believe it was to smother them under 40,000 cubic metres of slag.

I'm writing this after reading about an attack by Al-Shabaab militants in Kenya. They attacked a university near the border with Somalia. One hundred and forty-seven people died, most of them Christians, who were singled out and deliberately killed.

I don't believe that was God's plan. Before that, I was reading about Andreas Lubitz, the Germanwings pilot who deliberately flew himself and his passengers into a mountainside in the Swiss Alps. I don't believe that was God's plan either.

When I preach in churches, I look out over the congregation and, whether I know the details or not, I'm aware there are people sitting there who've known grief and pain. Some have been divorced and they don't see their children. Some are childless and it's a continuing, unassuageable ache. Some are in physical pain. Some have lost parents, friends, or siblings, far too young. It is not God's plan.

I know that very few people reading this are going to say outright, "Yes, it is." We would rather talk about God's preferential will – what he *desires* should happen – and his permissive will, what he *allows* to happen. Or we'll talk about human freedom, and how so many of the bad things that happen to people are the fault of human beings in the first place, and if they'd made better choices they wouldn't be in the mess they're in. Or we'll admit that we've made bad choices ourselves: that we're partly responsible for that marriage breakdown, or that we failed at work because we were lazy and irresponsible.

All these things are true. So why do we still talk about God having a plan, if we need to do all these mental gymnastics before we can bring ourselves to believe it? How does it work, if his plan can so easily be buffeted around by other people's choices or our own inclinations? Why are we so desperate to hang on to an idea that has so little going for it and which seems to force us to believe in a God who does really terrible things to us?

Is there a better, biblical way of understanding how he works in our lives? I believe there is. I think we're more faithful to the totality of what God says in his word when we stop saying that he has a plan for our lives. In many ways, that's a hard call. It's something that evangelicals have grown up with. It was in the old hymns:

> *I know who holds the future, and he'll guide me*
> *with his hand,*
> *With God things don't just happen, everything by*
> *him is planned...*

(Alfred B. Smith & Eugene Clark, 1947)

It's hard to let go of it. But we should, because it does us no good.

Let's acknowledge, first, that people have different accounts of God's plan. One of them arises from a particular theology, which is generally called "Calvinist". Let's call this the "hard" version. In this one, God's sovereignty is understood as meaning that he orders everything. In one of his sermons, based on Isaiah 46:10b ("My counsel shall stand, and I will accomplish all my purpose"[ESV]), John Piper puts it like this: "God has the rightful authority, the freedom, the wisdom, and the power to bring about everything that he intends to happen. And therefore, everything he intends to come about does come about. Which means, God plans and governs all things."[1]

Behind this is a grand vision of the might and majesty of God, who has no equal, whose power and wisdom are unlimited, and who is not only the creator but the sustainer of life. There's much in this to applaud. If God is not omnipotent and omniscient, he is not God. But there's a huge jump from saying that God *can* intervene, shape, and direct everything that happens in the world to saying that he *does*. And if we claim that he does, we're ultimately saying that God has deliberately chosen everything, the good and the bad.

In this view, we have to put up with bad things happening to us because it's ultimately for our own good, just as a child has to put up with a measles vaccination. In some unspecified and incomprehensible way, we still have free will and moral agency. But, ultimately, the awesome power and majesty of God overrule and overwhelm: all we can do is resign ourselves to his will, trusting that it is good and perfect.

There's an anonymous poem that sums it up, comparing life as we know it now to the reverse of a tapestry, in which the pattern is obscured and barely discernible. So:

> *Not till the loom is silent*
> *And the shuttles cease to fly*
> *Shall God unroll the canvas*
> *And explain the reason why.*
>
> *The dark threads are as needed*
> *In the Weaver's skilful hand*
> *As the threads of gold and silver*
> *In the pattern He has planned.*

In other words: the bad things that happen to you are God's doing and part of the masterwork he's making of your life.

Alexander Pope wasn't a Calvinist, like John Piper, but he put it this way in his 1733–34 *Essay on Man*:

> *All nature is but art, unknown to thee,*
> *All chance, direction, which thou canst not see;*
> *All discord, harmony not understood;*
> *All partial evil, universal good;*
> *And, spite of pride, in erring reason's spite,*
> *One truth is clear, Whatever is, is right.*

But, often, what is, is wrong. Some things that happen are just too terrible to justify by talk of dark threads or universal good. If we're to believe that God plans the tsunami, the cancer, Islamic State, what's required of us is not just a leap of faith, but a total suspension of our moral judgment. And "Woe to those who call evil good and good evil, who put darkness for light and light for darkness, who put bitter for sweet and sweet for bitter," says Isaiah (5:20, NIV).

God does not plan evil. Yes, of course, he allows it. He's created a world in which human beings have freedom to hurt as well as to help. He's created a world in which fire burns as well as warms, water drowns as well as sustains, tectonic plates shift and cause earthquakes and tsunamis as well as lifting land masses out of the sea to provide a place for us to live. What else was he supposed to do?

But when we talk about God having a plan for our lives, we aren't talking about what he allows to happen because the world is as it is. We're talking about him having his hand on my life, directing it this way and that – to this job, this life partner, this church, this ministry. We're talking about him choosing that one person should suffer pain and another should not, that one should succeed and another fail, one live and another die – and the sick, the failures, the bereaved are supposed to accept that this is right because God has chosen it.

Now, ultimately, if we push logic to its Calvinistic limits, God wills anything that he does not choose to prevent. But when logic seems to drive us to a conclusion that's at odds with everything we feel and know about the God we're being logical about, it's time to think again. We can believe in a God who's all-good, all-loving and all-powerful, and accept that he chooses not to swat the mosquito that will give us malaria or tweak the gene that gives us cancer. But when we use the language of the "plan" – a personalized programme that's just for us – we've gone beyond what the Bible says and we're offending against our God-given sense of justice.

That's not to say that we can't see how pain can work for our good. Things happen to us that are very, very hard. When we've come through to the other side, we can sometimes look back with thankfulness and see what we've learned: we're better, wiser, stronger, more loving. Athletes who want to become stronger put their bodies through punishing training regimes. The way they build up their muscles is by damaging them. Go to the gym, lift the weights, work out on the machines, and you'll feel the pain. That pain comes from microscopic tears in the muscle fibre. When your body heals them, your muscles are bigger and stronger than before. Your spiritual pain serves the same purpose: it makes you strong.

And that's right. We learn through the things that go wrong – or that we do wrong. We can get stronger through things that cause us pain, and wiser through things that baffle us.

But that's a world away from believing that God plans our pain. I think the idea that God deliberately weaves dark threads into our lives is theologically flawed and psychologically cruel. I think we should stop saying it and start offering people something more real, more exciting, more dangerous, and more true.

Taking the Bible seriously, though, doesn't mean that we have to accept that view of how God works in the world. There are plenty of thinkers around today who have pointed out its logical and theological limitations. "Open theists" such as Clark Pinnock in his 2001 book *Most Moved Mover* have argued that God leaves the future "partly settled and partly unsettled". In his chapter "The Scriptural Foundations", he writes: "God does not manipulate the creature and does not micromanage the universe. The term 'sovereignty' is not synonymous with 'all-controlling'."

For Pinnock and others, freedom is real, not imaginary. He goes on: "We are not asked to believe that God exercises all-controlling sovereignty and still holds human beings morally responsible. The Bible is coherent and the contradiction is imaginary. All-controlling sovereignty is not taught in Scripture." It may not be taught in Scripture, but it's assumed in much of the language we hear about "God's plan". And, whether you sign up to the whole "open theism" package or not, it doesn't work.

It's not this "hard" version of God's sovereignty that's the most pernicious, though. The "soft" version runs like this: God wants us to be happy and fulfilled. To ensure that this happens, he's created a personalized route map for our lives. If we follow it, all will be well. If we don't, we can expect consequences. It's like a reward for solving a crossword puzzle. Just Google "God's plan for my life" if you don't believe me.

This is the product of a fundamentally materialistic and consumerist world view in which it's normal for good things to happen to us. Religion is a spiritual investment that pays temporal dividends. When things are going well, it seems to work: that's God's plan, after all. When they aren't, it's not so clear. Either "God is testing us", in a coolly experimental process designed to make us stronger and better people, or we've sinned in some way and departed from his perfect will and it's our own fault. If that's the case, the plan has failed. But the language survives: shorn of any relation to real life, the idea that God has a plan still grips Christians who haven't been taught to think of their relationship with him in any other terms.

Where does the idea that God has our lives mapped out for us come from? There are plenty of Bible verses cited in its defence. But when these are looked at carefully, we see how slender is the evidence. It's often related to Jeremiah 29:11, for instance: "'For I know the plans I have for you,' declares the Lord, 'plans to prosper you and not to harm you, plans to give you hope and a future'" (NIV).

But read it in context, and you will see that God is talking to the exiles in Babylon in the time of King Nebuchadnezzar. How does a verse written to a specific group of people in the sixth century BC get to be preached as God's personal message to the twenty-first-century Christian worried that he hasn't got that promotion at work yet?

Or there's Exodus 4:11 (ESV): "The Lord said to Moses, 'Who has made man's mouth? Who makes him mute, or deaf, or seeing, or blind? Is it not I, the Lord?'" Or Psalm 139:13: "You formed my inward parts; you knitted me together in my mother's womb." Of course: God is our creator; we owe him every breath that we take. What other way could the biblical writers have chosen to express their sense of utter dependence on him?

Or what about Isaiah 29:16 (NIV), where the prophet compares human beings to clay jars made by a divine Potter: "Shall what is formed say to the one who formed it, 'You did not make me'? Can the pot say to the potter, 'You know nothing'?" (Paul quotes him in Romans 9:20.) But, like the rebuke delivered to Job by God (Job 38 – 42), this is the prophet asking mortals the question: "Who do you think you are?" Before God, nothing.

There are other verses that speak more directly of God's intervention. When Joseph confronts his brothers about their treatment of him and they're terrified of his revenge, he reassures them by referring to the purposes of God: "As for you, you meant evil against me, but God meant it for good, to bring it about that many people should be kept alive, as they are today" (Genesis 50:20, ESV).

Isaiah also speaks of Cyrus, the Persian king who allowed the Jews to return home from exile: "From the east I summon a bird of prey; from a far-off land, a man to fulfil my purpose. What I have said, that I will bring about; what I have planned, that I will do" (46:11, NIV).

There are many other verses that speak of his working behind the scenes to bring about a particular result. None of these need to be denied or explained away. History is his story: what God has planned, he will do. But not everything is planned. God does not have a plan for your life, or for mine.

The trouble is that all too often verses like these have had a weight put on them that they can't possibly bear. So we're forced into all sorts of mental gymnastics to try to justify the idea that God has a plan for each individual, even when this idea so clearly fails the test of experience.

"There has to be a plan. I have to believe that."

And that's the problem: take away the idea that God is in control of everything that happens, and the alternative is too terrifying to contemplate. At its worst, what we're left with is a God who is a heartless game-player. As Edward FitzGerald put it in his translation of the *Rubaiyat of Omar Khayyam*:

> *Tis all a Chequer-board of Nights and Days*
> *Where Destiny with Men for Pieces plays:*
> *Hither and thither moves, and mates, and slays,*
> *And one by one back in the Closet lays.*

There's another way of looking at it, though. Suppose that, instead of trying to map a philosophical determinism or a spiritual consumerism onto the Bible, we actually read it? When we do that, we don't find the God of the philosophers and scholars or the God of the shopping mall. We find the God of Abraham, Isaac, and Jacob. We don't find that God plans our future. We find that he accompanies us into it. "Even though I walk through the valley of death, I will fear no evil," says the psalmist. Why? "For you are with me, your rod and your staff comfort me." God doesn't give us a predetermined route map to follow: he walks with us as we find out the way for ourselves.

I believe we'd be spiritually healthier if we dropped talk of God having a plan for our lives, and started talking about God having a hope for our future – a hope that's ultimately based on resurrection. God's hope for our future is about second chances, about choices and new beginnings. It's about forming us into the kind of people who make the right choices, because we've been shaped by Christian fellowship, prayer, teaching, and discipline. It's about making us into people who'll be faithful in adversity, not because we believe God is deliberately testing us or inflicting pain on us for some ulterior motive, but because we believe he is able to save us to the uttermost.

I believe this idea of God is far closer to the God of the Bible. In the Bible, the picture we have is one of human freedom, held in dialogue with divine action. Humans act, and sometimes they do well, sometimes badly; God responds, in loving mercy or in judgment.

God calls, to a new place, a new venture, or a new understanding: humans respond, with incomprehension, with delight, with obedience or disobedience. He isn't moving pieces around a draughts board. He's involved in a relationship. He's not a logician; he's a lover. And he's a lover who never, ever gives up on the beloved, no matter what the disappointments or the failures in the relationship might be.

Does he have a plan for us? No. At every stage of our lives we're faced with decisions. Usually these are at a practical level. What career should I choose? Should I go to college or university? Where should I live, where should I go to church, how much should I spend on my holiday, what's the best mobile to buy? Whom shall I marry, if anyone?

We make decisions all the time. Even this kind of decision is fraught with spiritual implications. How we spend our money is a moral issue. How far we please ourselves instead of paying attention to other people's claims on us is a moral issue too. What our education and career choices say about our values matters. And there are other choices that we recognize more easily as being between right and wrong: what will we choose when we're faced with choices about sex, about honesty, about integrity? Every one of these choices shapes our future. Every one of them – some more than others – provides the opportunity for a right turning or a wrong one.

If God has a plan for my life, it means that I have to work out which is the right one. If I get it wrong, what happens to the plan? Does it exist in some sort of potentiality, which my bad choices mean I can touch on or glimpse occasionally but never fully realize? And, if that's true, what sort of plan is that, and what does it say about the sovereignty of God? We can do better than that.

God's hope for my future means that within each wrong choice there are right choices to make – and his desire is for me to flourish, within the context in which I find myself and according to my capacity, and above all for me to become more Christlike. I don't need to be rich, or healthy, or admired, for that to happen. I don't need to believe that my life is on invisible rails that are carrying me to a destination that's been predestined for me.

I don't need to covet the shiny future offered by televangelists who tell me that God wants me to be prosperous and happy, with a loving wife and 2.4 children who are all walking with God. I just need to know that, whenever I do wrong, or when wrong is done to me, or things just go wrong – and they do, that's just life – I'm never abandoned, and God still wants me to learn, grow, and flourish as far as my circumstances will allow.

Morally, I might commit all sorts of sins – and I have. They don't fit into the "plan" idea, either: but I know God has never given up on me. So every time I take the wrong path at a fork in the road, I know I'll come to another fork before long. Again, there'll be a choice: and the more wrong turns you take, the harder it becomes to do the right thing, but it's never impossible with God as your guide.

Ultimately, our hope rests in the resurrection of Jesus. When Jesus rose, it was God's statement that hope never ends. There are an infinite number of second chances, because God is infinitely loving and merciful. I don't believe God has a plan for my life. But I believe that he has a desire for me, to be filled with his Spirit and made Christlike, and that, if I'm faithful and prayerful, he'll show me how to be all that I can be.

John Milton (1608–74) was one of the greatest of English poets, and his greatest poem is *Paradise Lost*, which tells the story of the creation and fall in twelve books of blank verse. It has some marvellous passages in it, but it's fair to say that it can be quite hard going.

Get to the end of it, though, and there's a wonderful image. Adam and Eve have failed and forfeited their place in paradise, there's an angel with a fiery sword preventing them from ever returning, and they're facing a future of hard work and pain of a kind they've never experienced before. But the poem doesn't end on a note of bleak tragedy. It ends with hope:

> *Some natural tears they dropped, but wiped them soon;*
> *The world was all before them, where to choose*
> *their place of rest, and Providence their guide.*
> *They, hand in hand, with wand'ring steps and slow,*
> *through Eden took their solitary way.*

They have lost one life, but God has not abandoned them: the world is all before them, where to choose... And, in their exit from paradise, there's a sense that they are growing up, taking responsibility for their actions, learning, and changing. Their spiritual muscles have been damaged and torn. But they'll heal, and they'll be stronger for it. The tears dry, the eyes brighten, the hope rises.

We all lose our Eden. Some of us might feel we never had it. But God's hope for our future means we never run out of choices. He doesn't have a road map for our lives, but that doesn't mean there isn't a destination.

1 www.desiringgod.org/sermons/the-sovereignty-of-god-my-counsel-shall-stand-and-i-will-accomplish-all-my-purpose

2

God doesn't heal everyone, and he doesn't want to

A few years ago I went to an art exhibition in London. It wasn't a pretty sight, but then it was by Damien Hirst, who made his name by pickling dead animals in formaldehyde, so I knew what I was getting into. There were twelve bloodstained glass and steel cabinets crammed with medical glassware, surgical implements, weapons, and apparently randomly chosen objects lining two of the walls. Each had a pickled bull's or cow's head in front of it.

On the other two walls were collages made of dead butterflies and an arrangement of glass shelves surmounted by a dead dove, in front of which was another tank with nothing in it. Upstairs were four more severed heads, stuck full of knives, scissors, and shards of glass.

Each of the twelve cabinets represented the martyrdom of one of the apostles, the shelves with the dead dove were the Ascension, and the empty tank was Jesus. The butterfly pieces were called *Hope* and *Pray*. The heads upstairs were the Gospel writers – each tank contained a commentary on one of the four. So, was it random blasphemy, just a way of poking fun at Christianity? Was it perhaps just a bit satanic? It's Damien Hirst, after all – some people think he's brilliant; others think he's having a laugh at people with more money than sense.

Well, I surprised myself. I came away very thoughtful, thinking that, actually, Hirst probably was brilliant after all, and that I'd seen something really important. I couldn't decipher all the apostles' cabinets – maybe they just didn't have any hidden meanings – but St John's contained a lighted candle and a monkey's paw. The candle symbolizes eternal life, perhaps referencing the legend that grew up that John would not die until Jesus returned (John 21:23), and the monkey's paw is a reference to the 1902 horror story by W. W. Jacobs in which a monkey's paw grants an old couple three wishes (let's just say it doesn't turn out well, and gave me nightmares when I read it as a child).

The lesson is, be careful what you wish for. Whatever life promises you, it will be dust and ashes in the end. Even the beautiful butterfly collages were only possible because of the creatures' deaths. And those gospel-animals stuck full of blades, what were they? Revenge on the writers for misleading the world, as Hirst might imagine? Or just a symbol of how human wickedness can wreck even the most beautiful visions and ideas?

I don't know, but since then I've thought about it quite a bit. I think Hirst was expressing a view of life and death that was frightening, nihilistic, and tragic, and I think the only way he could find to do that – his only partner in dialogue, if you like – was Christianity, because Christianity deals with the deep, dark, tragic things in a way that's utterly honest.

I don't think that makes him a Christian, but I do think he might be a prophet. I think that in a society obsessed by health, wealth, image, choice, and personal gratification in every area of body, mind, and spirit, Hirst was looking for a language in which to say, "Actually, it isn't really like that" – and found it in the Bible. It's in the Christian Scriptures that he sees a raw honesty which allows the depth of spiritual response he seeks. There wasn't a specific image of crucifixion in that exhibition, but there might as well have been. For Hirst, the whole world's crucified.

What's missing is hope. There's no resurrection, no sense that Christ is a living saviour. It's not Christian, it's sub-Christian; it's the negation of faith, hope, and love. Jesus said: "The thief comes only to steal and kill and destroy. I have come that they may have life, and have it to the full" (John 10:10). This is death and destruction, not abundant life.

But maybe we need to let that challenge us. I admire the courage with which Hirst, and people like him, face the world as it is. In T. S. Eliot's memorable phrase, they see the skull beneath the skin. I wonder if Christians – at least in the comfortable West – are as brave. It's tragically easy for Christians to sell out to a fundamentally secular vision. We may put a religious twist on it but what we end up offering is sub-Christian too. It's not the whole gospel because it doesn't have the cross.

I have a friend who is disabled and has a generally low quality of life. Not himself a believer, at a particularly low point he was taken to a "celebration" evening by two Christian friends who thought he needed to be blessed. Standing on either side of him, they forced him to join in the worship by taking an arm each and raising it in the air.

On one level, this is an example of spiritual abuse. On another, it seems to me, it stands as a metaphor for that sub-Christian approach to problems, including the problem of suffering, in general. Rather than truly acknowledging the sadness, frustration, and pain that characterize the lives of all too many people and asking what God is saying through these things, we just try to fix them.

In one way, that's fair enough. Care for other people is built into the DNA of our Christian faith. Jesus said: "I was hungry and you gave me something to eat, I was thirsty and you gave me something to drink, I was a stranger and you invited me in, I needed clothes and you clothed me, I was ill and you looked after me, I was in prison and you came to visit me" (Matthew 25:35–36, NIV). That's been a template for Christian social action ever since. How could we not care for people when Jesus commands us to do so? But here's the danger. What happens when we can't fix stuff?

The last century has seen a technological explosion the like of which the world has never experienced before. The world of a hundred years ago is at once tantalizingly close, through family traditions and early film records, and startlingly alien. Take, for instance, one of Britain's great air pioneers, Sir Thomas Sopwith (1888–1989). He learned to fly in 1910 and went on to develop one of the most successful aeroplanes of the First World War, the Sopwith Camel, built of wood and canvas. He lived to see supersonic jets, moon landings, aircraft carriers, jet packs, and the vertical take-off and landing of the Harrier jump jet.

In every field of human endeavour, progress has been extraordinary. Agriculture, transport, communications, construction – you name it, we have far, far outstripped our ancestors. In medicine, we can answer questions about the human body and what goes wrong with it that previous generations hadn't even thought of. We can cure diseases they didn't have names for. We can routinely save people's lives from diseases that were fatal – a hundred years ago a simple infection could be a death sentence.

And what about poverty? In the last twenty years, nearly 1 billion people have been taken out of extreme poverty, as countries have grown richer. Nearly three-quarters of them live in China. The resources that are available to us to improve people's lives, to help and heal, are vast. But what happens when our solutions don't work? When we can't solve people's problems with money or technology, when we can't blame them for being the authors of their own misfortunes, and when even our prayers don't seem to achieve anything?

When I was being educated for Baptist ministry, one of my lecturers – himself a minister of vast experience – told us to prepare for this. He said: "There will be times when you're walking up the path to a house, knowing that behind the door there's a situation you can't do anything about. And, at the end of the visit, you'll walk down the path knowing that you've made no difference at all."

Now, usually, I believe ministers do. I've often taken comfort from the words of another pastor, who said: "We do far more good than we think we do, and we do far less harm than we think we do." But still: there are lost sheep who are just lost, prodigal sons who never find the way home, and sick people who are sick all their lives and then die. More than that: there are people who are emotionally and psychologically damaged, too, and never find the fullness of life that Jesus spoke of. And it's not that they won't, or they might do if a counsellor were better at her job, or if the church's worship band was up to scratch. They just can't: the wounds are too deep. So what does the church do with people like that? Here's the thing.

Christians rejoice when the sick are made well, but curing the sick is not the purpose of Christianity. Christians rejoice when the poor are made prosperous and the hungry are fed, but relieving poverty and feeding the hungry are not the purpose of Christianity. Christians rejoice when scientists uncover more of the mysteries of the universe – as Johannes Kepler said, "thinking God's thoughts after him" – but the advancement of learning is not the purpose of Christianity.

Whenever we adopt someone else's agenda, no matter how praiseworthy it is in itself, we're being faithless. Peter defined the church like this: "You are a chosen people, a royal priesthood, a holy nation, God's special possession, that you may declare the praises of him who called you out of darkness into his wonderful light" (1 Peter 2:9, NIV).

That's where our discipleship starts and finishes: not with achieving a particular task, but with bearing witness to Jesus. Yes, of course Jesus healed the sick and cared for the poor. But: most of the sick in Israel he did not heal. Most of the dead he didn't raise. Most of the poor were still poor. Based on the sort of measurable outcomes that people working in health and social services today require, Jesus' ministry was a failure. But I believe that this "failure" has as much to teach us as his "successes". Because the truth is that Christianity can't solve every problem. We can't fix everything that's wrong. We can't make everyone happy.

If we're honest, or if the problem before us is too difficult to be wished away, we might admit that Christians face heartaches and pain just like everyone else, but our default position is that God makes everything better. And we do love those stories of redemption. For a couple of years I was the editor of an evangelistic magazine designed to introduce people to the

Christian faith. Among other things we ran stories of hope, about people whose lives God had turned around. They'd found faith, or found strength through the faith they already had, or through the support of God's people in their church community. They'd come off the drugs, they'd kicked the alcohol habit, and they were faithful Christians, doing their best.

I believe all those stories. Sometimes I read about what had happened to those people and how their lives had changed, and I had to blink the tears out of my eyes. That's not to say that they were restored to what they were. I remember one woman whose drug use had so incapacitated her for motherhood that her children were taken from her. She's now clean, working to help other women who are in the same situation that she was twenty years ago. It's a success story. At least, up to a point; because this lady has never seen her children again.

I believe passionately in hope. There's no one who is beyond God's reach. But I think we need to be more honest than we sometimes are about suffering. Not all of it is redemptive: it doesn't always make people kinder or wiser. Some people's lives are so vandalized, either by the actions of others or just by how things turn out for them, that they'll always be marked by their experiences.

It seems to me that many Christians have enormous difficulty accepting this, and this places intolerable burdens on those who already have enough weight to bear. So, for instance, why isn't a sick child healed of a terrible genetic condition? You'll sometimes hear people saying it's because their parents haven't prayed hard enough or faithfully enough. That just adds another layer of pain to the sadness and frustration they already feel.

And it's because we don't accept the obvious: Jesus didn't heal everyone. Today, genuine miracles are rare, and we have no reason to expect anything different. In spite of the claims of "healing ministries", God does not usually step in to cure someone of cancer. In our heart of hearts, we know this. When I was in pastoral ministry, I found that when people – including myself – had to pray for people who were seriously ill or dying, we found it much easier to pray that God would give them spiritual strength than that they would actually get better. In other words, we believed that God could more easily adjust a mental reality than a physical one.

At some stage I realized that those prayers were made in bad faith. It's not that some things are "easier" for God to do than others – he's God, after all – but that we find it easier to conceive of God changing minds than changing the behaviour of cells. Is it just faithless to admit this? Of course not. It doesn't mean we don't believe in miracles. A Christian doctor, who's closer to these situations than anyone else, doesn't stop praying for her patients because she knows what's likely to happen – though she might pray a bit differently.

But it does mean that we're left with that question: what do we do with people God doesn't heal or help? Who are damaged, struggling, in pain, and who are going to stay that way? These people aren't success stories and don't find their way onto the front page of an evangelistic magazine. I wonder if they're an embarrassment – people to be written out of the victory script because they don't quite fit the church's image. But they are children of God too, loved by him as much as the healthy, happy, golden poster child for Christianity's marketing department.

The existence of people who are sick, disabled, and damaged within the church is very, very challenging. Not because they make us question the goodness or the power of God – though they may – but because they make us ask how we can see these people not as lacking something, part of Christ's body on sufferance, but as fully and completely a part of it as the happiest and healthiest Christian imaginable.

And here we go back to the crucifixion. What we've done, in our modern, fix-it-all way, is to imagine that the resurrection of Jesus fixed the crucifixion. Yes, it was terrible, but Jesus was raised, so everything's OK.

Well: up to a point. But that's not exactly what the New Testament says. In John's Gospel, the wounds of Jesus are still visible on his resurrected body: John 20:19–20 (NIV) says: "Jesus came and stood among them and said, 'Peace be with you!' After he said this, he showed them his hands and side." In other words, the scars are still there. Later in the chapter, we're told that Thomas wasn't there with the rest of the disciples and refuses to believe that they've seen Jesus. Jesus appears and says to him (verse 27): "Put your finger here; see my hands. Reach out your hand and put it into my side. Stop doubting and believe."

In Revelation 5:6, John sees "a Lamb, looking as if it had been slain" – that is, sacrificed, with the wounds still visible. Once someone has been crucified, they may be resurrected but they cannot be un-crucified. So the risen and ascended Christ carried his wounds into heaven. The body of Christ on earth, the church, is wounded too.

In a tremendous leap of spiritual imagination, the hymn writer Matthew Bridges (1800–94) wrote in his great Ascension hymn: "Crown Him the Lord of love,/ behold His hands and side,/ Those wounds, yet visible above, in beauty glorified." But how can the wounds of God's people be glorified in beauty?

Some years ago the World Council of Churches produced a report about the theology of disability, entitled "A Church of All and for All". It asks serious questions about the sort of church Christ calls us to be. It says in paragraph 28: "If Christ is the true image of God, then radical questions have to be asked about the nature of the God who is imaged. At the heart of Christian theology is a critique of success, power, and perfection, and an honouring of weakness, brokenness and vulnerability." A little later it says: "Without the full incorporation of persons who can contribute from the experience of disability, the Church falls short of the glory of God, and cannot claim to be in the image of God."

That paper is talking specifically about physical disability. That's really important, but we live in an age in which huge efforts have been made to bring physically disabled people into the social mainstream where they belong. Most of us take it for granted now that having limited vision or mobility or hearing shouldn't stop you taking part in things. That's not to say that we've arrived, either as a society or as a church, but at least we know what we ought to be doing.

But what applies to physical disability applies equally to emotional, psychological, and spiritual disability. So what does the Christian community have to offer to those who are not well, in mind, body, or spirit? I think there are three things.

First, an acknowledgment of the dark and tragic element in Scripture. I don't know how many of us would preach on the book of Joshua and grapple with themes of genocide and ethnic cleansing (Joshua 6 – 8, 10:29–43); or Noah's ark, and really face the horror of the story of a world that perishes by water as we fear the destruction of the world in a nuclear holocaust (Genesis 7:23); or Jephthah's chilling story of human sacrifice (Judges 11); or Lot's offer of his virgin daughters to the raging mob outside (Genesis 19). I wonder, even, how often, other than on Good Friday, we preach about the crucifixion.

It seems to me that there's room for this darkness in our sermons and Bible studies. After all, God is not, if we are to be true to Scripture, the chilly abstraction defined in the Westminster Confession of Faith (1646) as "without body, parts or passions".

Most of us aren't philosophers of religion – though if we are sensible, we'll respect the work that Christian philosophers do in making it possible to talk about God in the most rarefied spheres of language and logic. Most of us need to be able to talk about God as a person, who is always beyond us, but not so far beyond us that we can't relate to him. We find the language of faith and experience not in the lecture hall but in the Bible: and those stories are often troubling, dark, and distressing.

A few years ago, the atheist philosopher A. C. Grayling wrote a sort of alternative to the Bible, which he called *The Good Book* (Bloomsbury, 2011). It's divided into different "books" including Genesis, Wisdom, Parables and Lamentations, and draws on authors throughout the ages who Grayling thinks had useful non-religious things to say about life. Most of the reviews weren't very positive.

One of the noteworthy things about it was how it excluded those dark and difficult stories from the real Bible. There's no crucifixion. But if we leave those things out of our Bible we may actually be toning down the power of the God-story for those who need it most and who simply want something that expresses their suffering. And because the stories are biblical stories, God is in them – even if he is not a God with whom we might feel particularly at home. So preachers need to learn to preach on those things, not in a way that lessens the tragedy at the heart of them, but in a way that recognizes it and still finds hope and good news.

Second, we can offer teaching about suffering that helps people do more than just endure it. There's a rich historical seam of spirituality and theology that modern Protestants have forgotten about but which speaks of the value of suffering. The martyred Archbishop Oscar Romero once said: "There are many things that can only be seen through eyes that have cried." That's not the same as saying that suffering is to be welcomed, or that God deliberately chooses to inflict it on people. Neither is it to say that suffering, of the mind, body, or spirit, is always a path to some kind of enlightenment: as the Catholic philosopher George Santayana wrote, "If pain could have cured us we should long ago have been saved."

Nevertheless – and this is something to say in fear and trembling – suffering can be a gift. There are hints of this in the New Testament. Paul says in Philippians 1:29 (NIV): "For it has been granted to you on behalf of Christ not only to believe in him, but also to suffer for him" – note the word "granted", the word used for a favour. In Colossians 1:24 he says: "Now I rejoice in what I am suffering for you, and I fill up in my flesh what is still lacking in regard to Christ's afflictions, for the sake of his body, which is the church." Both refer to suffering for the gospel. But other kinds of suffering can be gifts as well.

In John 9 we have the story of Jesus' healing of the man who was born blind, one of the seven "signs" in John's Gospel. It begins: "As he went along, he saw a man blind from birth. His disciples asked him, 'Rabbi, who sinned, this man or his parents, that he was born blind?'

"'Neither this man nor his parents sinned,' said Jesus, 'but this happened so that the works of God might be displayed in him.'"

The disciples reflected the common view of the time, that disability was a consequence of sin. But Jesus turns this on its head: what counts is what God is able to do in this person's life. Make no mistake: suffering can be destructive. But it can also teach us to pray, to sympathize, and to look outwards instead of being consumed by our disadvantages.

One of the great evangelistic hymns of the church is "Just as I am". It was sung for years at Billy Graham rallies and has probably accompanied more souls into the kingdom of heaven than any other. It was written by Charlotte Elliott in 1835. She became an invalid at the age of thirty, once writing, "My Heavenly Father knows, and He alone, what it is, day after day, and hour after hour, to fight against bodily feelings of almost overpowering weakness and languor and exhaustion, to resolve, as He enables me to do, not to yield to the slothfulness, the depression, the irritability, such as a body causes me to long to indulge..."

She was converted after meeting a minister named César Malan at a supper with friends. Malan asked if she were a Christian; she put him off. But later she said to him, "I want to come to Jesus, but I don't know how."

"You have only to come to him just as you are," said Malan: and the hymn was the result. Whatever our lot in life, we come to him just as we are, not as we might have been if things had been different: and eyes that have cried see things to which others are blind.

Third, we need to identify what we can offer that is good for people who are damaged in some way. In part this rests on an acknowledgment that we cannot necessarily make them better. However, this is a long way from saying that a Christian community can't offer anything but a stiff upper lip.

Alison Webster, in her book *Wellbeing* (SCM, 2002), suggests this: "The opposite of wellbeing is not illness, but dis-ease, in the sense of unease – being ill-at-ease with ourselves. Wellbeing is not the result of 'cure' but of the incremental building of networks of relationships and human connection, self-esteem, self-belief, purpose, meaning, value and good relationships."

If you think that this is a pretty modest aim for the church, you'd be right. But I suspect that many of us can recognize in that quotation from Alison Webster a description of what actually happens in our churches. Because the church is not always there to provide solutions to problems. Much more often, it's to act as a moral landscape that is rich enough and varied enough for everyone, healthy, sick, and damaged, to find their own place and still know that they belong – and that, in spite of their limitations, that world is still held within the loving purposes of God.

That Damien Hirst exhibition was intended to be deeply offensive. So is the gospel. There is nothing offensive about saying, "We have a product that will make you happier and healthier." But it is, I suspect, rather offensive to say, in the twenty-first-century UK, that happiness and health are not attainable for everyone, that providing them is not God's priority, and that we will take up the cross of Christ and follow him anyway.

3

Beginning at the beginning: Why we need to talk about origins

I interviewed someone who had just started working for a major Christian organization in a significant leadership role. Among other things, I asked about the pressure points for evangelical Christians today. I wanted to get at the things we disagreed about and which might make unity in a common purpose more difficult. What about creationism, I suggested. How old, give or take a few million years, did he believe the earth was? He gave a delightfully non-committal answer, which proved the point of the question: creationism has become something that we're reluctant to discuss, because we might offend someone.

When we first meet a fellow Christian and start getting to know them in a way that delves below the surface, we sometimes find ourselves trying to decode their theological language. Do they think like me? What are the red lines of their personal faith, and do they match mine?

One of these might be where they stand on the young-earth creation question. Is it an article of faith, right up alongside the Trinity? Is it one of the *adiaphora*, the issues on which Christians are legitimately allowed to differ without being branded as heretics? Or is it just bunk, the quaint survivor of a pre-scientific age which has no more scientific validity than the belief that the earth is flat?

It's a genuine issue. An email survey of 628 Evangelical Alliance members in 2008[1] asked people to complete this sentence: "The best explanation for the origin of humans is..."

It elicited the following responses:

- 66.6 per cent said "special creation created by God on the sixth day"

- 15.3 per cent said "intelligent design"

- 16 per cent said "Darwin's theory of evolution made possible by a creator God"

- 2.1 per cent said they did not know.

Creationism – shorthand for the belief that the world is only a few thousand years old and that the first three chapters of Genesis are strictly historical – has traction. This is less the case in the UK than in the US but, according to the EA's research, at least, it's still a big thing. In many churches it's assumed to be gospel truth, and defended – sometimes passionately – as such. In many others it just isn't discussed.

Maybe the age of the earth and the mechanism God used to create it, and to create us, have become something we can chivalrously agree to disagree about, like baptism and bishops and the role of women. Or maybe it's become such a dividing line in evangelicalism that we don't dare to talk about it any more, like my interviewee.

If there are things we can't talk about, it's troubling. And I do wonder how many preachers in the evangelical world are prepared, publicly and unapologetically, to come down off the fence and preach full-blooded, passionate, committed, and informed sermons on the first few chapters of Genesis.

Here's the problem. If we just avoid the subject, in home groups or sermons or discipleship and evangelism classes, we're shutting ourselves off from a rich, deep, textured treasury of story and meaning. Our gospel preaching is lamed, because we can't preach the new creation with understanding if we haven't grasped the old. The whole Bible is ours. If we're honest, some parts of it are more useful than others. But it is all the inspired word of God, and Genesis has enormous resources for us.

We all come at this from a particular point of view. I grew up in a church that taught six-day creationism. We had expert speakers from scientific backgrounds who put the case against evolution. It was presented as a simple choice: either you believed the Bible or you didn't.

It was a large church that tended to be all-absorbing for a young person, with very few opportunities to interact with people from different traditions. While on one level questions were encouraged, the answers were always pretty cut and dried. If Jesus is not Lord of all, he is not Lord at all, we were told. It's not an expression I use today. The trouble is that it lends itself too easily to a subtle but intense pressure to conform. It's sincerely meant, but the "all" of which Jesus has to be Lord too easily becomes "my package of doctrines and codes of behaviour". Anyway: at some point I realized that I didn't believe in young-earth, six-day creationism any more. It just seemed clear to me that the Genesis accounts were a different type of literature and that reading them as history made as much sense as trying to follow the plot of a maths textbook. It just doesn't work that way.

For some evangelicals, particularly in America, that view is just anathema. It was recently reported that a jawbone found in Ethiopia was 2.8 million years old and might have belonged to one of our earliest human ancestors. Franklin Graham, a major evangelical public figure, son of Billy Graham and founder of the Samaritan's Purse charity, took to Facebook with a passionate proclamation: "If you really want to know where our original ancestors came from, check the original source: God's Holy Word. The Bible clearly tells you – they were created by God. The first man was Adam and the first woman was Eve."

I don't want to engage here with the scientific arguments against young-earth creationism. But I do want to say this: God gives us minds capable of investigating the deepest things of creation. Physicists and chemists can fathom the movement of the stars, the currents of space, the composition of the elements, and the nature of the fundamental energies of the universe. Geologists can identify the composition of the earth over the aeons of deep time since it came into existence. Biologists can describe the process by which organisms develop and become adapted to their environments, such that some flourish and some fail.

If the world was created in six days a few thousand years ago, it means that they are all wrong. Because all their learning leads them to the same conclusion: that the universe started with a Big Bang nearly 14 billion years ago, and that we are the product of countless generations of evolution.

I'm very comfortable with the idea of individual scientists and theories being wrong and particular disciplines being blind alleys that have to be abandoned. That's how science works. And

I don't think that just because lots of people believe something, it has to be true. But neither do I believe that God is a deceiver. I think he wants human beings to follow where the evidence leads. And if the evidence led to young-earth creationism, it would have been demonstrated by now. In fact, scientifically minded people who want to hold on to a young-earth theory can only do so by increasingly desperate special pleading.

G. K. Chesterton, the great Christian thinker, wrote this in his story *The Curse of the Golden Cross*:

> *Tell me that the great Mr Gladstone, in his last hours, was haunted by the ghost of Parnell, and I will be agnostic about it. But tell me that Mr Gladstone, when first presented to Queen Victoria, wore his hat in her drawing-room and slapped her on the back and offered her a cigar, and I am not agnostic at all. That is not impossible; it's only incredible. But I'm much more certain it didn't happen than that Parnell's ghost didn't appear; because it violates the laws of the world I do understand.*

The question was never about what God could do. Of course he could have created the world in six days. The question is, did he? The answer has to be, no. So what about Genesis 1? If we say that it's not a science or a history book, we don't diminish it. We restore it to its proper place, as a passionate, engaged, revelatory piece of theological writing. This is how it works.

The Bible begins with a picture of chaos, a nothingness waiting to become something. For the Hebrews, the sea was sometimes used as a picture of the chaos that was opposed to

God's order. So we might imagine it as a sort of surging sea, without waves or water, but there is nothing that language can do to help us much.

The creation begins with God saying, "Let there be light." Again, we can imagine this as we like, but it is a dramatic moment. In Haydn's *Creation*, the moment is captured with a choir singing softly, "And there was..." and then exploding on the word "LIGHT" with a great fanfare and crashing chords from the orchestra. There is a New Testament reference to this verse that has awe-inspiring implications. In 2 Corinthians 4:6 (NIV) Paul says: "God, who said 'Let light shine out of darkness,' has made his light shine in our hearts, to give us the light of the knowledge of the glory of God in the face of Christ."

In other words, the glory of the birth of a universe, in which God brought order into a chaotic nothingness, is matched and mirrored in our own rebirth. Job 38:7 pictures the angels shouting for joy at the creation; Jesus tells of the joy in heaven over the one sinner who repents. We should not take the miracle of conversion lightly.

Verses 6–10 of Genesis 1 speak of the formation of the land and sea. The groundwork is done on which an inhabited world will be built. The Hebrews had no concept of space. For them, the world was an island of stability in a watery chaos. God makes an "expanse" to separate earth from water; it is a dome over the world, and without it we would be engulfed.

It isn't water on the other side of the sky, but space – we've been there. But there is a profound truth in the Genesis story. This is a "Goldilocks" world: not too hot or cold, with gravity not too great, and an atmosphere hospitable to life. In a universe with billions of stars, it may be the only one. Ralph Waldo Emerson wrote, "If the stars should appear one night every thousand years, how would men believe and adore; and preserve for many generations the remembrance of the city of God which had been shown!" Perhaps: but we would more probably be terrified.

Isaac Asimov, the science fiction writer, wrote a story called *Nightfall*, about a world in a solar system with six suns. Its inhabitants have never seen the stars, so have no reason to believe they exist. Once every few thousand years, all its suns are eclipsed at once, revealing that Lagash is in the heart of a mighty cluster. Traumatized by the knowledge of their insignificance in the universe, they become insane.

But the biblical writers, more aware perhaps even than we of the fragility and sheer unlikeliness of life on earth, are moved not to fear or despair, but to praise: "Lord, our Lord, how majestic is your name in all the earth!" (Psalm 8:9). God has created, and God sustains, the world. It exists because he wills it, and so do we.

Once the shell of the world was in place, it had to be made habitable. God begins with the basics, the greenery. The repeated formula "according to their kinds" is aimed at the paganism of surrounding people. This story was written for a society that knew its reliance on seedtime and harvest. A bad year spelt hunger, starvation even. Even when everything had been done right, bad weather or a plague of locusts could wipe out the work of the whole year. Life was random. But the gods who controlled the weather and the growth of the corn could perhaps be influenced by sacrifice and offerings – ever more costly, and perhaps more brutal: human sacrifice was common enough.

In Genesis, the picture is of an orderly world, which is set going by God, and then creates itself. It is not capricious. God doesn't need to be bribed by sacrifice before he makes the rain fall and the grass grow. Right at the beginning of the Bible we are taught about grace, and about freedom: God is not the sort to force people into obedience.

Verse 14 deals with the creation of the sun and moon – only they aren't called that, but "two great lights"; and in a throwaway line, it says: "He also made the stars." They aren't called the sun and moon because in the cultures of the time those were also the names of the deities associated with them; it would be like saying, "God created Ra" or "Apollo", which would be confusing at best.

The stars were studied because they were thought to foretell the future. The clear skies of the desert lent themselves to stargazing, and astrologers learned the intricate movements of the heavenly bodies. Surely they had a meaning? If so, it was only for the gifted few who had the time and skill to find it out. But the writer of Genesis 1 says, "These are just lights. They are not gods and goddesses. God made them for our convenience; you should not worship them."

In Psalm 8, the poet refers to the heavens as "the work of your fingers, the moon and stars, which you have set in place" (verse 3). It doesn't even take any effort; this is the work of God's fingers, not his "mighty arm". The stars are God sticking sequins on the sky.

All this tells us that we can live free from fear. Our lives are not controlled by the stars. We are not at the mercy of powerful gods and goddesses. Everything we see is made by the same hand, and while not everything goes right for us, it isn't because the gods are angry.

There are modern versions of this fear that our lives are shaped by forces beyond our control. Sigmund Freud taught us that we don't really understand our reasons for feeling and thinking what we do. Karl Marx taught us that our small decisions are part of vast movements in economics and politics, of which we are barely aware. Charles Darwin taught us that we are the products of millions of years of evolution; our animal origins shape our behaviour today.

But if anyone says that we are controlled or defined by psychology, or economics, or evolution, Genesis 1 says, "No. These are part of God's world, and we don't need to fear them." The gods aren't angry; the answers are not written in the stars. We're free.

In verses 20–25 the author continues his great assault on paganism. Ancient peoples were not as prone to dividing the world between natural and supernatural, or physical and spiritual, as we are. The natural world was alive in a way that's strange to us now, and it was perilous. Sea creatures were inhabitants of the world of chaos; woods and forests were dark wildernesses that contained fierce beasts. There were lions in Israel and Judah.

But Genesis 1 says again, "God made all of these – the birds, sea creatures, animals wild and tame, are under control. They are not extensions of some hostile spirit. They are good."

This fear of wildness runs very deep in us, though wilderness is enjoyable enough to visit. The Greeks had legends of the god Pan, who would terrify shepherds and travellers; our word "panic" comes from this: it is what happened when you encountered Pan. But, in today's world, that fear of nature is likely to be replaced by something worse. We are so technologically advanced that we can do whatever we like. We can move mountains and change the course of rivers. We are nature's masters – or, at least, we think we are.

But we are not as wise as we think. We have the technology,

but not the wisdom to let us use it well. We know enough to act, but not enough to stop. In 2015 Pope Francis wrote a marvellous encyclical – technically a letter to his bishops, but really aimed at the whole Catholic Church – in which he spoke of the relationship between human beings and the world they live in. *Laudato si'* ("Praise be to you", a quotation from St Francis of Assisi) calls for an end to the "throwaway culture" of overconsumption and waste. It warns against an ideological refusal to accept the reality of climate change. It says that the poor suffer most in the pursuit of profit at any price.

Among other things, Francis says: "A spirituality which forgets God as all-powerful and Creator is not acceptable. That is how we end up worshipping earthly powers, or ourselves usurping the place of God, even to the point of claiming an unlimited right to trample his creation underfoot." And, he says, we can't carry on as we are. He writes of "the lie that there is an infinite supply of the earth's goods, [which] leads to the planet being squeezed dry beyond every limit".

Genesis tells us that the world is not ours to do with as we like. It has been given – and if we love and respect someone who gives us something, we cherish the gift as a reflection of what we feel for them.

Then, when God has created the world and furnished it with plants and animals, he makes people – "in his own image", it says (verse 27). What does this mean? Certainly not that we are like God in any physical sense. It's helpful to think about what we know about God so far: not much, other than that he is a creator. He brings order out of chaos. So, at this point, we know that people are creators too. We are part of creation, but set aside from it; we can make things, and change the world.

So creativity, the ability to affect our environment, is built into us. This has all sorts of implications. It says something about our political systems: dictatorships that deny people freedom or justice are attacking the image of God. If you have no autonomy, you are less godlike. It says something about poverty: if people are so poor that they lose any sort of choice about how to live, the image of God is destroyed; if we have no way of affecting outcomes, we are not creators any longer. It says something about work: if people have to toil at a job they hate because they need the money, and can't go home at the end of the day satisfied that they have done something worthwhile, the image of God is denied. All of these things take away freedom and joy.

There is a deep desire in us for freedom. We are made in God's image, and denying freedom is denying our nature. Churches are not very good at this. We tend to over-control what people think and do. But perhaps God worries less about things like that than church leaders and theologians.

So the idea that God creates human beings in his own image is a very rich one, especially in this Genesis context, and even more especially compared with the sort of ideas about God that were around at the time. In one version of the Babylonian creation myth of Marduk and Tiamat, Tiamat was the primordial chaos monster who gave birth to sea serpents and storm demons. Marduk kills her by smashing her skull and cuts her in half. From her ribs he makes heaven and earth; her weeping eyes become the sources of the Tigris and Euphrates, and her tail the Milky Way.

In Greek mythology, the Titan Kronos devoured his children, fearing that they would overpower him. The infant Zeus was spirited away and raised to adulthood, returning to vanquish his father. In Norse mythology, Odin killed the giant

Ymir and created the world from his dead body. His blood was the sea, his flesh the earth, and his skull the sky.

So, in many creation stories, the world is made in hatred, through violence. These things are built into the fabric of life, and into the earth itself: it is how the people who told these stories saw their own nature and the nature of the world. But, in Genesis 1, people are made through God's word. No one dies, and we're told "God blessed them". The refrain throughout the chapter is "God saw that it was good", and at the end of his creating it says: "God saw that it was very good."

Stories shape us. Stories about origins shape whole cultures. Imagine the difference between a culture that believes, right down at its deepest roots, that human beings came into existence because of an act of murder, and a culture that believes human beings came into existence because of an act of love.

Evangelical Christians have a strong doctrine of original sin. But we have been much less interested in exploring the doctrine of original goodness, which is so clearly taught in the first chapter of Genesis. With all that we have done to spoil the world, and with all the wrongdoing that blights human relationships, the world is a good place because God made it so. There is goodness in the heart of every human being, no matter how far they have fallen. If this weren't so, they would be unable to respond to God's grace, and we cannot believe this is true of anyone.

And then the writer of Genesis 1 makes a point of saying, "male and female he created them". Gender is there at the very beginning of creation, but there is no sense that man or woman is privileged one above the other. This is a verse that has been reclaimed in modern times by those who argue that men and women are equal in every sphere, and this is fair enough. But those who originally wrote it during the Babylonian exile may not have had such elevated views, and this is rarely how it's been understood in Christian history.

The verse has more often been used to argue for the status quo in gender relationships, whatever that might be at a particular place and time: that there are roles appropriate for men and for women. Every society seems to develop these ideas, and they always have the capacity to become oppressive. We need to be very wary about letting Scripture be used to justify them – so that preaching is "male" and teaching Sunday school is "female", for instance.

Worse: as I write, there has been a series of violent attacks in Washington on transgender people, men and women who feel that they're in the "wrong body" and don't choose to dress or act according to their apparent gender. The legal rights and status of these people is being fought through the courts in several US states, amid very bitter rhetoric. Christians do wrestle with this issue and there are complex questions of psychology that test the understanding of even professionals in the sphere to the limit. But using these words in Genesis as a way of prescribing how people ought to feel and behave isn't particularly helpful. Perhaps we should simply accept that the words cannot bear all the weight that's sometimes put on them. "Male and female he created them" is a statement of fact; it's up to us to work out what this means, with all the wisdom and kindness of which we're capable.

Men and women are then commanded to "fill the earth and subdue it", to "rule over the fish, the birds and the living creatures". This is a command that has been used to justify all sorts of activity. We can do what we like to animals, for instance, because God says they are ours to rule over. The environment doesn't matter, and we can drill for oil where we like and poison rivers with chemicals – God says we are to subdue the earth. Some people even argue that it's wrong to try to limit the population because we are commanded to "fill the earth". All this is very misguided. The writer is simply continuing the theme of God bringing order out of chaos. We are God's agents in this. And while nature is self-regulating to a great extent, it needs to be controlled in order to make it hospitable to human civilization.

One of the reasons we enjoy wildernesses is that we are not faced with a daily struggle for survival. In our own country, before eighteenth-century tourists discovered that the English Lake District and the Scottish Highlands were sublime, they were seen as terrifying. Sensitive souls even used to have themselves blindfolded before traversing the wild crags and mountains. Nature was to be tamed; in its raw state, it was not enjoyable at all. Genesis was written in that context: gardens were better than wildernesses. But gardeners are creators, not destroyers.

It's interesting too that in the beginning everything was vegetarian, even lions and tigers. The Genesis writers knew that predators – including humans – ate meat. They were from a society that could not afford to be sentimental about animals. They lived closer to nature than we do, and killing to eat was natural. But they seem to have had a deep sense that, in a perfect world, no one would kill anyone or anything. Isaiah 65:25 looks forward to the restoration of this primal harmony: "'The wolf and the lamb shall graze together; the lion shall eat straw like the ox, and dust shall be the serpent's food. They shall not hurt or destroy in all my holy mountain,' says the Lord" (ESV). This is a challenge to Christians, who are to live now in the light of the coming kingdom. We should kill as kindly as we can, and perhaps as little as we can; and animals are to be cared for, not harmed.

With the opening verses of Genesis 2 the first account of the creation comes to an end. God has worked for six days and now he "rests". We have not felt, as we read, that he has been working particularly hard. A world has come into being not by some titanic labour, but by six words; six times God said: "Let there be..."

Nevertheless, at this point there is a pause. In the notional history of which Genesis is a part, the Sabbath rest has not yet been instituted; this is a long time before the Exodus, in which the Sabbath is first formalized. But we can be as sure as we ever can about such ancient texts that this Genesis account was written when the Sabbath rest had become a fundamental part of the religious life of God's people. It is fitting, then, that God should finish his work with rest.

At one level it might be argued that the story is shaped this way to reinforce a sort of social control. Priests have a vested interest in maintaining the status quo, and telling people that God himself kept the Sabbath is a powerful incentive for them to keep it too. This is fair enough, but it does not really do justice to the integrity of the story. It makes much more sense to say that Sabbath is what happens in a society that is ordered correctly, where people live rightly and in harmony with God and with each other. So for God to rest at the end of a working week fits the fundamental pattern of spiritual life for his people – and because the story is set when it is, it becomes the template for that pattern.

Over time, Sabbath-keeping, with circumcision and to a lesser extent dietary requirements, became one of the distinguishing marks of Jewishness. Because Christians tend to "read" Judaism through the lens of the New Testament, which majors on the points at which Jesus comes into conflict with Jewish tradition, we can end up with a very jaundiced view of Sabbath-keeping – though that has not stopped many Christian traditions being quite as strict as first-century Pharisees in this respect. And because evangelicals tend to read the New Testament through the eyes of Martin Luther, who preached the importance of grace, we often hear it said that Jews tried (and try) to "earn their way to heaven" by keeping the Old Testament law, including keeping the Sabbath.

This is not how they saw it, or see it. They were very much aware of the grace of God, and keeping the law was their response to it. Of course this could lead to abuse, and we are familiar with some examples from the New Testament. But there is no reason to think that Jesus did not keep the Sabbath himself, or that he encouraged his followers not to.

He did, though, teach that "the Sabbath was made for man, not man for the Sabbath" (Mark 2:27). In other words, we should look to the deep structures of the law and apply them for the benefit of human beings, rather than imagining that we please God by chaining ourselves to the meaning of every letter. So what does the Sabbath mean today? In many ways, this day on which God did nothing is the most significant of all. It is a radical assertion of human freedom. It says that we are more than just producers and consumers of goods. It opens the door to whole worlds of human culture: to art, music, and literature, as well as to spirituality.

In many underdeveloped societies (though we should be careful about describing them in a way that implies that development as we understand it is the desirable norm), life is a daily battle for survival. Food insecurity is a fact of life. However much we might sometimes like to romanticize life in a "state of nature", the truly poverty-stricken are probably better described by Thomas Hobbes in *Leviathan*: their lives are "solitary, poor, nasty, brutish, and short".

For many people today, setting aside one day on which no work is done is an impossible luxury. Nevertheless, God says that this is how it is to be. So the Sabbath can be seen as a way of saying that everyone is to have enough to eat, and to spare. The daily bread for which Jesus taught us to pray is not to be just enough to keep body and soul together. It is to be enough to allow us to flourish in mind and spirit, as well as in body.

Without leisure, we are slaves to our physical needs, like those of whom Dr Johnson wrote in *The Rambler* that they "see the sun rise with no other hope than that they shall fill their bellies before it sets".

The technological revolution that began with widespread industrialization in the nineteenth century has, for the first time, freed millions of people from the fear of not knowing where their next meal is coming from. To say that this gift is unequally distributed is an understatement. We are kept too well aware of the realities of life for many in developing countries by aid agencies and journalists to think otherwise or to romanticize the lives of the very poor.

But the idea that what the world needs is for everyone to be like us ought to be critiqued as well. The strength of Sabbath-keeping lies in the fact that it is part of a spiritually balanced pattern of life. The Sabbath offers rest in the awareness that work and rest are both gifts. If it is cut loose from its moorings, leisure drifts into spiritual danger.

We see this in the enormous growth of the leisure "industry" and the explosion of ways to pass the time. Three television channels have become hundreds. Phones have become mobile computers. Computers have become indispensable providers of information and amusement, and they make it very easy to shop. The touch of a few keys can bring us whatever we desire, and so we do our bit for the economy by spending money on what we might well be able to do without.

Again, it would be foolish to deny the benefits of all this or to wish it were otherwise. I write these words on an iPad on a train journey from London. If I want to check a fact, I can go online and do it. The spiritual danger, though, is that instead of being enslaved as producers, we become enslaved as consumers. The virtual world is often brighter and more exciting than the real one. It asks less of us, and it seems to offer a great deal more.

No one wants to legislate for Sabbath-keeping, and we are instinctively, and rightly, repelled by the thought of those Scottish outposts of Sabbatarianism where the children's swings were chained up on Sundays. The underlying theme of this opening chapter of Genesis has, after all, been freedom. But, in a truly modern irony, keeping the Sabbath might mean not just controlling our work, but controlling our play.

What I've tried to do in this chapter is move the debate on Genesis 1 away from whether it's history or not. It isn't – it's much more exciting than that. It's how God teaches us who we really are, and how we fit into the world he's made. The tragedy of making it a battleground in the war over biblical orthodoxy is that we stop reading it and preaching it for what it really is.

1 21st Century Evangelicals, www.eauk.org/snapshot

4

Evangelism is not about saving people from hell

When I was a young minister, my church took part in a community mission with other local congregations. It lasted a week and we called it "Who Cares?", which we thought was very clever and thought-provoking – God cares, that's who. As it turned out, the local people didn't, and it was all a bit of a flop. Our events weren't all that well attended, and when they were it was by people who already went to church. So it sometimes goes.

There were nine churches in our patch, in varying states of congregational health. The biggest was the parish church, which attracted several hundred and had room for more. Mine, just the other side of the cricket pitch where W. G. Grace used to play, was usually fairly full, often with over a hundred present. The others were smaller, some of them with huge buildings and small congregations rattling around inside.

But here's the interesting thing. As part of our preparation for the mission, someone with a yen for statistics worked out the population of our electoral ward. He also added up the seating capacity of all our church buildings combined. The result has stayed with me and made me think very hard about the whole evangelism and church-growth thing. Because he found this: if every seat in every church was occupied on a Sunday – and that's the sort of thing that gets Christian media really excited about revival – it would still leave 95 per cent of the local residents not in church.

To underline: if that beautiful Methodist chapel with the huge, empty gallery went from a congregation of thirty to one of 500, it wouldn't, in the broad scheme of things, make the slightest difference. If the fiercely independent Brethren assembly went from fifteen on a Sunday to 250, maybe the extra offerings would help it fix the roof, but that's about it: in terms of the number of people whose lives were actually transformed by the good news of Jesus, it's insignificant. So what is evangelism about?

I think we need to admit that if it's about the traditional evangelical concern – saving people from hell – it's pretty ineffective. Yes, it's possible to argue that if there's no room for 95 per cent of the population in church, we should build more churches – and church-growth strategists say that starting new churches (though not necessarily putting up new buildings) is actually a very good way of making more Christians.

But, even back in the days when we like to think most people did go to church, it turns out that most of them didn't. On census Sunday in 1851, an estimated two-fifths of the population was in church. According to Professor Robin Gill (*The "Empty" Church Revisited*, 2003), churchgoing in England for the Anglicans and Congregationalists peaked relative to population in the 1850s and for the rest of the Free Churches in the 1880s, with continuous decline ever since. Even on the very questionable assumption than everyone in church was a Christian and everyone outside wasn't, that still leaves an awful lot of people heading for the hot place.

The aim of this book isn't to offer an intense biblical study of Christian doctrines complete with Greek, Hebrew, and pages and pages of footnotes. Its purpose is to name the things that we don't talk about, or that we assume without thinking about, and to offer ways of talking and thinking about them that are a bit more honest. Evangelism is one of them.

Evangelicals are evangelical – the clue's in the name. "Evangel" means "good news" – the Greek word for "angel" or "messenger" is in there. "Gospel" means the same in Old English. The word "evangelical" has cut loose from its original meaning. It's used to describe anyone who's enthusiastic, passionate, and committed. You can be evangelical about stamp collecting or rambling. (It's also, in an uncomfortable and inappropriate twist, become a noun – the badge of a party rather than the mark of a disciple.)

But what is the good news that we are evangelical about? What do we think we're doing when we're persuading people who aren't Christians to commit themselves to following Christ? And, if we admit – as we surely have to – that we're never going to fill every church to capacity, and that, even if we did, the vast majority of the population still wouldn't attend – what counts as success?

Let's acknowledge, first of all, the elephant in the room. There are plenty of Christians who believe – uncomfortably and apologetically, perhaps, but they believe it – that the gospel is about saving people from hell. If you aren't a Christian, you're going to face an eternity of torment/separation from God/annihilation – the consequences of unbelief are variously understood, but they're all pretty unpleasant. So the good news we offer is that when someone turns to Christ, they are literally saved from a fate worse than death.

I confess I wonder about that. The idea that God would deliberately create millions of human beings in the knowledge that they were hellbound – because the vast majority would either never hear the gospel in the first place, or if they did would never respond to it – is counter-intuitive, for a start. And leaving the eternal destiny of others up to human beings, who as we all know are inclined to be more than a little lazy, foolish, impatient, and often just not very bright, hardly seems fair.

In our "Who Cares?" mission, the person supposed to be responsible for administration and publicity was me. I was terrible at it. The idea that someone's eternal salvation might have depended on my getting publicity out in time for them to arrange a babysitter is terrifying.

Of course, many people reading this will do so with a sense of pity that anyone could still be troubled about such a primitive doctrine. God is love, they'd say, adding variations on the theme of "I can't believe that he would send anyone to hell."

However, the fact that I don't personally like an idea doesn't matter too much, not if I want to be serious about discipleship. The Bible, and with it "the faith once for all entrusted to God's holy people" (Jude 3, NIV), is not an à la carte menu: you get what you're given. The argument from personal incredulity is never very strong. Yes, you can say that the biblical writers were just wrong, and that they had misunderstood or misreported Jesus if you like – but, however we understand the doctrine of the inspiration of Scripture, cutting loose from the Bible like that is probably a step too far for most readers.

I think there are a lot of people like me. We don't like the idea of hell and we want to preach the goodness of God, but we don't talk about it. That's because, at least in some circles, if we do, we run up against an orthodoxy that will not allow questioning. One person who exemplifies this is Gregory MacDonald, who wrote an excellent book entitled *The Evangelical Universalist: The Biblical Hope That God's Love Will Save Us All* (2006). The book does what it says: it's a rigorous, detailed, thoroughly biblical case against the doctrine of eternal punishment. But here's the thing: Gregory MacDonald is not Gregory MacDonald at all. He is Robin Parry, a biblical scholar who when he wrote it was the editorial director of Paternoster, a well-known evangelical publishing house.

He wrote under a pseudonym for two reasons: first, as he says in the preface to the second edition, because "if word got out that the head guy at Paternoster was a universalist then our market and our authors would not see things so sympathetically", and, second, because he'd written another book, *Worshipping Trinity: Coming Back to the Heart of Worship* (Lutterworth, 2013), which was more important to him and which he didn't want to compromise by seeming like a heretic. So he set up an email account and ran a website in Gregory's name. (He even did a radio interview about the book with his voice disguised to sound like Darth Vader.) Parry only admitted his real identity three years later, in a blog post on 29 August 2009.

The story got plenty of publicity, and Parry realized that not just Paternoster but its parent company, Biblica, might suffer for it. He offered his resignation, which wasn't accepted (he pays generous tribute to Biblica's then CEO, Keith Danby), and left for other reasons a few months later. Parry experienced not only a professional conflict of interest but personal attacks – he says that "the actual trigger for the self-revelation was receiving the nth email in my Gregory email inbox accusing me of a lack of integrity and seeking to hinder proper academic debate".

Someone else who suffered this was the author and former megachurch pastor Rob Bell. As the pastor of Mars Hill Church in Grandville, Michigan, he had a hugely influential ministry, reaching out to people who were disconnected from traditional preachers and preaching. He became a popular conference speaker and narrated the influential NOOMA series of videos.

There was always a section of American evangelicalism that didn't take to Bell, regarding him as too liberal to be truly one of them. However, it was a book he wrote about hell in 2011 that tipped him, as far as they were concerned, into the enemy camp. That book was *Love Wins*. In it he says: "It's been clearly communicated to many that this belief [in hell as conscious, eternal torment] is a central truth of the Christian faith and to reject it is, in essence, to reject Jesus. This is misguided and toxic and ultimately subverts the contagious spread of Jesus' message of love, peace, forgiveness and joy that our world desperately needs to hear."

Without taking a position, he outlines various other views of what happens to non-Christians after death, including annihilationism (extinction) and universalism. Of the latter, he says: "Whatever objections a person may have to [universalism], and there are many, one has to admit that it is fitting, proper, and Christian to long for it."

Bell's book was met by a chorus of outrage from US conservative evangelicals. John Piper, the hugely influential Calvinist theologian and pastor, notoriously sent a three-word tweet: "Farewell, Rob Bell."

Not all evangelicals felt like that. For some, even Bell's tentative offer of a different way of thinking about eternity was liberating. But, though he denies having been forced out, he faced opposition in his own church, and a little while later he left to explore other forms of ministry.

Why is it so hard to talk about hell? Why has it become such a core part of evangelical identity that questioning it is seen as a betrayal? In fact evangelicals are beginning to rethink the idea of hell as eternal conscious torment. A recent *National Geographic* article highlights the rise of the annihilationist school, which argues that after death unbelievers simply cease to exist, and universalists like Parry.[1] But they're still swimming against the current. In my darker moments I think it's such a totemic, primary doctrine just because it's so difficult, and holding on to it is a mark of theological virility. But many people would point out, quite rightly, that it's a real theological question: there are parts of the New Testament that seem pretty unequivocal. It's not the à la carte; it's the set meal.

On the whole, I think people who preach and teach this really do feel bound to do so by their devotion to Scripture – though I think there are a lot more who put it in that "too difficult" box. But here's the thing. I don't think that many of them, even of the strictest Calvinist persuasion, in their heart of hearts, really and truly believe it.

If they did, they wouldn't sleep at night.

The story is told of the famous Victorian criminal Charles Peace, hanged for murder on 25 February 1879. He was escorted from his prison cell by the chaplain, who was reading aloud about the fires of hell. The story – and it may be no more than that – is that Peace burst out: "Sir, if I believed what you and the church of God say that you believe, even if England were covered with broken glass from coast to coast, I would walk over it, if need be, on hands and knees and think it worth while living, just to save one soul from an eternal hell like that!"

If we really believed in hell, the knowledge that millions of human beings – among them perhaps friends, family – our own children, even – would spend an eternity in torment would be too much for us to bear. Bereavements, bad enough anyway, would become unendurable. We'd live our whole lives in a state of horror. In fact, we don't – even those of us who claim the strictest orthodoxy.

We soft-pedal the doctrine, so that we believe it in principle while in practice we hope and pray and trust that God is bigger and better than we've been taught he is. He won't condemn those *we* love, at least. Or we get round it by switching off our imagination, sternly affirming that whatever God does is right by definition, because God is God, and that when we get to heaven we'll somehow stop minding that most other people are in hell. Either way, very few Christians feel the reality of hell on their pulses, in the same way that we sometimes experience the reality of heaven.

At the same time, we believe in evangelism, often passionately. We're prepared to put time, effort, imagination, and cash into it. We love to see growing churches. We believe in mission and missionaries. But I'm not convinced it's because we want to save people from hell.

Now, I'll admit it: I like Robin Parry's line of thinking. He critiques traditional ideas of hell on philosophical, moral, and biblical grounds. He offers really interesting readings of Jesus' parables of Dives and Lazarus (Luke 16:19–31) and the sheep and the goats (Matthew 25:31–46), the usual "clobber texts" of the argument. I think he makes a good case for evangelical universalism – "the biblical hope that God's love will save us all".

But my point isn't that we should all stop believing in hell. It's still the default position of the Christian church that our eternal destiny is fixed at death, and I think Parry is right to say that "to jettison such a long-standing and clear tradition is something that should be done cautiously and reluctantly".

However, I think that most of us are functional non-believers in eternal punishment. And whether hell exists or not, and whoever goes there and for how long, I don't believe that we need it to make us evangelize – or, indeed, to make us live as good disciples of a good Lord. John Calvin, no less – who could never be accused of softy liberalism – wrote in his *Institutes* (Iii2) of the Christian mind that "restrains itself from sinning, not out of dread of punishment alone; but because it loves and reveres God as Father, it worships and adores him as Lord. Even if there were no hell, it would still shudder at offending him alone."

What I want to ask is why we believe in evangelism – and the real question is not what God is saving people from, but what he's saving them *for*. But let's admit, first, that we have our own agendas, and that they aren't always very spiritual or honourable ones – although they are very human.

In the years I spent in full-time pastoral ministry, I had two churches. One was medium-sized, with about 150 members. During the nine years I was there we saw steady growth and the average age of the congregation dropped quite a bit.

My second church was much smaller, but that one grew, too. Neither was spectacular, but the trend was generally upwards.

I was quietly pleased. I'd like to say that it was because I was glad to see people coming to faith and growing in faith. That was true. But it's also true that it looked like success, and success is nice. When people start coming to our church in greater numbers, it means that they've seen something they like, and that makes us feel good. Maybe they like us.

Maybe they like me.

And more people coming means more people who agree with us. In a culture where it's quite hard to be a Christian, when we're often thrown on the defensive by a dismissive comment at work or the barbed contempt of a TV comedian, the more people there are on our side, the better.

There are worse temptations. This book is written in the UK, where churches are a lot smaller than they are in the US. Obviously, many churches there are just like ours, with a few dozen or a few hundred in the congregation. There are, though, around 1,600 Protestant "megachurches", with more than 2,000 attenders. The largest, Joel Osteen's Lakewood Church, has an average attendance of 43,500 – it would need a building as large as most Premier League football stadiums if they all went to the same service. There are also around 3,000 Catholic churches with more than 2,000, but the dynamic is very different.

The largest congregation in the UK is Matthew Ashimolowo's Kingsway International Christian Centre, with up to 12,000 at its main church every Sunday. That's pretty impressive compared to the church where I worship, which hits forty on a good day, but globally it's not really in the big league: David Yonggi Cho's Yoido Full Gospel Church in South Korea has around a million members.

Most of us, I suspect, quail at the thought of our church growing to be anything like that large. We'd hardly know anyone. And where would we park? But there's something about a large church that speaks of success. A large church has more money. It can buy more things. Its audio-visual equipment is out of this world, and so is its sound system. Its coffee is better.

The temptation if you're a churchgoer is to think, "I want to be part of that." And there may be good reasons. If you have a family and that big, exciting church has a huge youth group, maybe that is the place for you. But sometimes it's just the desire to be on the winning team. Ministers are vulnerable to this. I've heard personally of more than one church where the minister has declared it his aim (it's usually male ministers that think like this) to grow the church to a particular size.

In America recently, this ambition led to the downfall of a pastor with a powerful and effective ministry. Mark Driscoll was pastor of Mars Hill Church in Seattle. It grew from a handful of people meeting in a home group to weekly attendance of around 12,000 in fifteen locations. Driscoll deliberately set out to be different and to reach parts of the population traditional churches didn't reach, and he was successful.

But Driscoll wanted to build the largest church in the world and he became dominated by that goal. In 2014, an extraordinary story unfolded as witnesses testified to his controlling behaviour and outbursts of rage. Those who criticized him were fired. He was found to have contributed misogynistic comments anonymously to an online discussion board. He was found to have plagiarized parts of his books and used an unethical promotional scheme to boost their ratings.

He once said of his opponents in a meeting: "There is a pile of dead bodies behind the Mars Hill bus, and by God's grace, it'll be a mountain by the time we're done. You either get on the bus or you get run over by the bus." For those who got run over, there was the sense that, for the alpha-male church leader, winning was everything.

Mark Driscoll failed on an epic scale – his church closed at the end of 2014 – but every Christian, and every minister in particular, needs to beware of the temptation he faced. This sort of approach has nothing to do with the gospel or the kingdom of heaven. It's not for us to set targets for church growth, whether the methods we use to achieve them are honest or not.

So we need to be honest about evangelism, and careful. Of course we should be thoughtful and effective. But we aren't growing a business or recruiting people to a club. We aren't enlisting people into a garrison so that they can help us defend it against a godless world. In fact, it's not about us at all, and we need to acknowledge and purge ourselves of motives like these.

We are simply witnesses. We're called to tell a story and share an experience, which together will lead people into a deeper, richer, and fuller life, reconciled to God and in harmony with one another. In John 9 we read the story of Jesus healing a man born blind. It contains the best rationale for evangelism I know.

The Pharisees can't reconcile the fact of the man's healing with the evident unholiness of the one who had done it; he'd healed him on the Sabbath. So, in a moment that's almost as comic as it is profound, they say: "Give glory to God. We know this man is a sinner." He answers in words that should be engraved on our brains: "Whether he is a sinner or not, I don't know. One thing I do know, I was blind but now I see."

We tell what we've seen. We share what we know. The rest is up to God. So here's why I think we should be evangelical.

1. Because Jesus is true

In his book *Credo*, in which he goes through the articles of the Apostles' Creed one by one, the theologian Karl Barth (1886–1968) put it like this: "Here the hidden, the eternal and incomprehensible God has taken visible form. Here the Almighty is mighty in a quite definite, particular, earthly happening. Here the Creator himself has become creature and therefore objective reality."

God became human. That is at the heart of the Christian faith. It cannot be negotiated or explained away. It is what you believe if you are a Christian, and everything else about Christianity follows from that.

If we Christians are sensible, we'll be deeply respectful of other faiths. All of the major religions contain deep wisdom. Properly practised, all of them make people live better. The fact that we have our own faith doesn't mean that we have to be dismissive of or antagonistic towards things that other people believe.

But Christians believe something remarkable and exclusive: that God came to this human world *as Jesus* and not as anyone else. As John says in his Gospel: "The Word became flesh and made his dwelling among us. We have seen his glory, the glory of the one and only, who came from the Father, full of grace and truth" (1:14, NIV).

The scholar and poet Helen Waddell (1889–1965) wrote a famous historical novel based on the tragic story of the medieval theologian Peter Abelard. At one point, through one of her characters, she gives a vivid illustration of the meaning of the Incarnation. Thibault points to a fallen tree, sawn through the middle, and says: "That dark ring there, it goes up and down the whole length of the tree. But you only see it where it is cut across. That is what Christ's life was; the bit of God that we saw."

The astonishing claim made by the Christian church is that, in Christ, God himself became visible and tangible. He contained himself in a human being. As Paul says, "In Christ all the fullness of the Deity lives in bodily form" (Colossians 2:9, NIV). When we see Christ, we see God. What we know of God is interpreted and defined by Christ. When we look at Christ, we are looking at God in cross section.

As truth claims go, they don't come any bigger than that. And the task of the church is to interpret that truth to the world: to say, "If you are serious about wanting to know how to live well, and if you want to be sure that your life has an eternal significance, this is where to come."

I believe we should be evangelical about people wanting to know the truth.

2. Because church is good for us

We don't always think so. Sometimes our fellow Christians annoy us intensely. In my work in Christian journalism I've often been saddened by examples of Christians behaving badly. Often when Christians fall, it's because of sexual temptation. But we're vulnerable to plenty of other things too. I've had to cover stories of Christian leaders who have abused their power and thought they were too important to take criticism. I've written about leaders who were greedy, leaders who were prejudiced and unloving, leaders who have tried to cover up wrongdoing instead of exposing it. And those are just the pastors: anyone who's part of a church knows that it can be really, really hard to get on with fellow believers.

Famously, C. S. Lewis in his *Screwtape Letters* has his senior devil advising his young acolyte, Wormwood, that if he really wants to put his "patient" off church he should get him to notice the neighbours he generally avoids: "Provided that any of those neighbours sing out of tune or have boots that squeak, or double chins, or odd clothes, the patient will quite easily believe that their religion must therefore be somehow ridiculous."

But church is more than that. Church in its essence is a new community of people who have a special relationship with Christ; who are "in" him, as Paul repeatedly says. It's a community where we learn a completely different way of life. We learn that, to be really happy and complete, we have to turn away from striving to fulfil our own natural desires. Instead, we let ourselves be shaped by loving, attentive relationships with others, all in the context of loving attentiveness to God. And, astonishingly, we find that instead of Christianity narrowing our horizons, stifling our individuality, and forcing us into a dead conformity, it liberates us. In the slow, years-long process of discipleship, we're moulded into better people: kinder, more understanding, more forgiving, more generous – and more Christlike.

Of course, in the average congregation, there are people at every stage of development. Some older people are spiritual children. Some younger ones are saints. Some are not good advertisements for faith – though there's always the thought "What would they have been like if they hadn't been Christians?" But a church community that is truly attentive to God offers the opportunity for people to live a life fulfilled in body, mind, and spirit.

I believe we should be evangelical about offering people that new, precious life.

3. Because Jesus people make a difference

In 2009 there was an advertising blitz by atheist campaigners. Comedian Ariane Sherine had the idea in response to Christian advertisements on London buses. With support from the British Humanist Association and famous atheist academic Richard Dawkins, they wanted to raise £5,500 to put slogans on thirty buses in London for a month. In the end they raised more than £150,000 and the campaign ran all over the UK. The slogan was: "There's probably no god. Now stop worrying and enjoy your life."

I'm not sure it converted many people to atheism. But I had two problems with it. For one thing, it misunderstood how Christians live. God is not a source of worry, and he doesn't stop us enjoying life. More importantly, though, I thought it was self-indulgent and unambitious. The best slogan they could come up with in the absence of God was "enjoy your life". This in a world where 11 per cent of the global population is hungry,[2] 6.3 million children under five die every year, and more than 33 million people are living with HIV/AIDS. Since then the Middle East has erupted again with the rise of Islamic State, which treats everyone who doesn't subscribe to its perverted ideology with extreme savagery. In our own country, half a million desperate people needed food aid in only six months.[3]

"Stop worrying and enjoy your life"? Actually, most Christians do. But we're driven, too, by a knowledge that the world as it is isn't the world that God meant it to be. When we become followers of Christ, we sign up to his agenda. Jesus didn't feed all the poor or heal all the sick. But neither did he turn away from those in need. His mission was to body, mind, and spirit.

One of the greatest figures of the nineteenth and early twentieth centuries was William Booth. The founder of the Salvation Army, he knew that a gospel that wasn't for the body as well as the soul was only half a gospel. On 9 May 1912, in his last-ever address, old and ill, he spoke to 7,000 people in the Royal Albert Hall. His words were on fire. "While women weep, as they do now, I'll fight. While little children go hungry, as they do now, I'll fight. While men go to prison, in and out, in and out, as they do now, I'll fight. While there is a drunkard left, while there is a poor lost girl upon the streets, while there remains one dark soul without the light of God, I'll fight – I'll fight to the very end!"

Three months later, "God's General" was dead. Thousands of people filed past his body as it lay in state. Around 35,000 attended his funeral. They had seen something Christlike in his life.

Believing in God doesn't make us worry. It doesn't stop us enjoying life. But it means we cannot shut our eyes to the needs of the world. Maximilian Kolbe, the Polish priest who died in Auschwitz after volunteering to take the place of a man sentenced to be starved to death, once wrote: "The most deadly poison of our time is indifference."

I believe we should be evangelical about calling people out of their indifference and into Christ's service.

So what about the 95 per cent of people who wouldn't be in church even if every church were full? I don't think saving them from hell is a very good motive for evangelism. Telling them the truth, helping them to know Jesus, and encouraging them to change the world: that I can get behind.

1 *The Campaign to Eliminate Hell*, Mark Strauss www.news.
nationalgeographic.com/216/05/160513-theology-hell-history-christianity
2 www.worldhunger.org/articles/Learn/world%20hunger%20facts%202002.
htm
3 www.trusselltrust.org/mid-year-stats-2014-2015

5

Forgiveness is much harder than we think

On 7 July 2005, four Islamist extremists detonated bombs on three London Underground trains and a double-decker bus in Tavistock Square. They were the country's first-ever suicide attacks and were followed two weeks later by a series of other failed attempts. These did produce one other victim, however: Jean Charles de Menezes, a Brazilian who was mistaken for one of the attackers and shot dead at Stockwell Station by police.

In the 7/7 attacks, fifty-two people were killed and more than 700 injured. One of the dead was Jenny Nicholson, twenty-four, who had studied English and music at Reading University. She planned to marry her soulmate, James White, do a PhD, and become a mother. Her own mother, Julie, was an Anglican priest in Bristol. She resigned from her post nine months later, saying in a BBC interview: "It's very difficult for me to stand behind an altar and celebrate the Eucharist, the Communion, and lead people in words of peace and reconciliation and forgiveness when I feel very far from that myself."

She has since written about her experiences in the memoir *A Song for Jenny*, which was adapted into a moving BBC drama. She said at a BAFTA screening of the film: "I can't pretend I have much forgiveness in my heart for the person who took my daughter's life. I don't feel it's my right and privilege to offer forgiveness. The only person who can do that is my daughter, who is not here.

"All we can do is open our eyes and look at the world and meet humanity with humanity. I had to work within myself at not hating and I am quite honest about that fight, but I don't trouble myself to think about forgiveness."

Nicholson's grief was profound, but so was her honesty. She's seen further into the nature of forgiveness than many Christians do, and admitted that she can't manage it. However: though people might have felt sympathy for her at the time, there's no doubt that, for many Christians, her resignation was a kind of defeat. Forgiveness, after all, is what we do. Most Christians pray every Sunday: "Forgive us our sins, as we forgive those who sin against us", or one of its variants.

I wonder, though, how often we stop and think about what we're saying. I wonder whether we really understand what forgiveness means. I think it's a word that's often trotted out without a real understanding of its power – and its danger.

The English Bible translates more than one Hebrew and Greek word as "forgive". Hebrew words can have the sense of "cover", "send away", or "let go". Greek words can have the sense of "be gracious to", "set loose", or "send away". The Old English root of our own word has the literal sense "give completely" or "give up".

All this helps us to a certain extent, though aside from the words themselves there are cultural assumptions involved in understanding them that also have to be acknowledged. What we understand by the word "forgiveness" might be something different from what a Hebrew of the time of King David or a Jew of the time of Paul understood. And what Christians today learn from Jesus or from Paul about forgiveness might be very different from what our own wider culture understands by it.

Words are important, because they're how we think. But at a different level, words also express how we feel. And while we understand how we feel through words, those feelings are sometimes too strong and complex for words to contain. That's especially true when we've been hurt in some way, or when we feel that we've been part of a great injustice done to others as well. So how can we be true to what we believe the Bible teaches, but at the same time deal with the unruly feelings of rage and bitterness, and the desire to make someone else suffer as we have suffered? Or at least, to make them feel ashamed because of what they've done?

We have to have some way of containing or resolving what we feel, or it will destroy us. One way, of course, is revenge. This desire is as old as humanity. Cain killed Abel because he was mortified that God had seemed to favour his brother instead of him. The story in Genesis 4 lays bare the pointlessness of Cain's action and its terrible results. It's also a window into the consequences of lack of forgiveness.

It's sometimes suggested that "the Lord looked with favour on Abel and his offering, but on Cain and his offering he did not look with favour" (verses 4–5, NIV) because Abel was a shepherd and offered blood sacrifices and Cain was a farmer and brought fruit and grain: here is a prefiguring of the sacrificial system that was to be instituted in later years.

But that's not what it says. The story offers no reason at all why one brother's offering was acceptable and the other wasn't.

That's just how it was. The storyteller knows exactly how the world works: sometimes life goes well for us and sometimes it doesn't, and it isn't necessarily anyone's fault.

Life, from a human point of view, is sometimes cruel. Sometimes it's because someone has deliberately tried to harm us. Sometimes it's random. In each case, disappointment and anger can lead to a desire to lash out. Cain, unable to deal with his rejection, took out his rage on the nearest target: his brother, Abel.

Cain's meaningless revenge on Abel was the first step in a cycle of violence and hatred. When God confronts him with his sin, he first asks, "Am I my brother's keeper?" Cain intends the question to be sarcastic: "Is he an infant, who needs looking after all the time?" We, the readers, even so many centuries later, desperately want him to see a different truth: "Yes, you are responsible for your brother, and we are all responsible for each other."

For Cain, though, it's too late. In an expression of terrible sadness, God says to him, "What have you done? Listen! Your brother's blood cries out to me from the ground. Now you are under a curse and driven from the ground, which opened its mouth to receive your brother's blood from your hand" (verses 10–11). Cain becomes an outcast and a wanderer. His descendant Lamech is another killer, who boasts that it is harder to bring him to justice even than Cain (verse 24). It is the first song in the Bible and it celebrates a murder.

But the spiral of violence is broken. In Hebrews 12:18–24, the author paints a remarkable picture contrasting the old covenant given at Mount Sinai with the new covenant given through Christ. Of the old, given to those who came to a mountain "burning with fire; to darkness, gloom and storm", he says that "the sight was so terrifying that Moses said, 'I am trembling with fear.'"

Then he gives the joyful contrast: "You have come to Mount Zion, to the heavenly Jerusalem, the city of the living God..." (verse 22). And this loving portrayal of the blessings of the gospel ends with him telling his readers – as the climax of a wonderful piece of rhetoric – that they have come "to the sprinkled blood that speaks a better word than the blood of Abel".

"Listen!" says God to Cain. "Your brother's blood cries out to me from the ground." It cries out for vengeance. The blood of Jesus speaks a better word: forgiveness. What the Hebrew sacrificial system symbolized and enacted for so many centuries, restoring relationships, resetting the clock, making it possible for enemies to coexist, the sacrificial death of Christ achieved at the most profound level imaginable.

Forgiveness is built into the deep structures of the Christian faith. Forgiveness is a way of dealing with the feelings that arise from betrayal that is spiritually unnatural. But if we cannot forgive, we are hardly Christians at all.

Forgiveness is at the heart of the gospel. Here are some things the New Testament says about it:

"Forgive, and you will be forgiven." (Luke 6:37)

Be kind and compassionate to one another, forgiving each other, just as in Christ God forgave you. (Ephesians 4:32)

"For if you forgive other people when they sin against you, your heavenly Father will also forgive you. But if you do not forgive others their sins, your Father will not forgive your sins." (Matthew 6:14–15)

> *Then Peter came to Jesus and asked, "Lord, how*
> *many times shall I forgive my brother or sister*
> *who sins against me? Up to seven times?" Jesus*
> *answered, "I tell you, not seven times, but seventy-*
> *seven times." (Matthew 18:21–22)*

> *Do not take revenge, my dear friends, but leave*
> *room for God's wrath, for it is written: "It is mine*
> *to avenge; I will repay," says the Lord... Do not be*
> *overcome by evil, but overcome evil with good.*
> *(Romans 12:19, 21)*

But what is forgiveness? How do you achieve it? Here are some things that it's not:

- It doesn't mean that you have to become friends with the person who has injured you.
- It doesn't mean that wrongdoing is ignored or condoned.
- It doesn't mean that feelings of anger and bitterness magically go away.
- It doesn't mean that you trust someone again just as you trusted them before.
- It doesn't mean that you won't be hurt again.

That looks like a very negative list, and in some ways it is. But let's clear away some of the mistakes about forgiveness before we come to what it really is.

1. Forgiveness doesn't mean friendship

If someone has deeply hurt or offended us, we may be able to forgive them. In a church context, that might mean we can share Communion with them. Communication might be re-established. Maybe, if we've previously been friends, that friendship might grow back. Maybe, because God is gracious, enemies can find things in each other that they come to admire, and even like. But it may not work out that way, and we need to be told that that's all right.

Sometimes, church leaders place burdens on members of their congregations that are impossible for them to bear, because they ask things of them that Jesus never asked. Perhaps they really do want to help people flourish in their spirits. But alongside that can go a desire to create a congregation that conforms to an unrealistic standard of peace, harmony, and good fellowship. Anything that doesn't fit the norm is frowned upon. So people who've been hurt can come under tremendous pressure to make light of what's been done to them, to pretend that they're "over it", and to wear the mask of friendliness no matter how much it costs them.

But forgiveness and reconciliation are not the same. There can't be reconciliation without forgiveness, but there can be forgiveness without reconciliation. It's the difference between a handshake and an embrace. Sometimes a handshake is all that's needed and all we can honestly offer.

2. Forgiveness doesn't mean ignoring wrongdoing

In the wrong hands, the doctrine of forgiveness can be a deadly weapon, allowing evildoers not only to escape the consequences of their actions but to inflict even more damage. In my work as a journalist I have found examples of Christian organizations where serious allegations have been brought before managers about the behaviour of senior employees. Instead of the complainants being listened to, they have been urged to "forgive" the person who has injured them – often with the implication that it would damage the work of the organization they cared about if they pursued their claim.

Personal relationships are another area where forgiveness needs to be handled with care. It's common to find stories of women who've been subjected to physical or emotional abuse and been urged to "forgive" their attacker by well-meaning but dangerously uninformed pastors. Both men and women can use religious language for their own advantage, to twist what should be a relationship of mutual caring and respect into one of dominance and oppression. But what does forgiveness look like when the power relationships are so unequal? What does forgiveness look like when the person who's done wrong doesn't think they have, or when they take forgiveness for granted, or when they repeatedly abuse the gift that's offered?

3. Forgiveness doesn't always mean you feel better

Actually, people who forgive often do. There are countless stories of people who have held on to bitterness and rage for years, or even decades, and whose lives have been ruined by it. Many have testified to the joy and sense of release they felt when they were able to forgive and to let the hatred go.

Some astonishing stories have been collected by The Forgiveness Project, a charity that brings together stories of people who've learned to forgive and cross bridges after unimaginably terrible experiences. It's not a religious charity, though some of the participants relate their forgiveness to their faith. Contributors include a survivor of Norway's Utøya massacre, Jews and Palestinians who have lost family to the other side, victims of violence and abuse – and perpetrators, too. Many of them speak of a measure of healing after they have forgiven.

The family of Jean-Baptiste Ntakirutimana from Rwanda were murdered in the 1994 genocide. In April 2008 he met the man who killed his mother, by then in prison. After a devastating conversation, he left with both of them "totally transformed". "I had gone there to help him, but in fact I had got more from the visit than I would ever have personally expected," he says. "As I left, it was as if I was carrying only half my weight."

Others, though, say that forgiveness is complicated. Another contributor, Jayne Stewart, who was abused as a child by her father – who continues to deny it – says: "Forgiveness is an interesting concept in relation to my father. I think forgiving is an ongoing process, which comes and goes and develops over time, rather than something that can be achieved once and for all..."

And this, too, we can understand. When Peter asked Jesus how many times he should forgive – seven times? Jesus answers: "I tell you, not seven times, but seventy-seven times." We assume that Jesus means seventy-seven separate offences. It's an extreme way of saying that there's no limit to the number of times we ought to forgive.

But maybe he's also acknowledging that there's no limit to the number of times we might have to forgive the same offence. What has been done to us keeps coming back: the memory of injury or betrayal rises in our minds again, for the second or the tenth or the fiftieth time, and each recollection requires a fresh act of forgiveness.

4. Forgiveness doesn't mean that you have to trust someone again

Yes, it may. Relationships can be restored so completely that they are stronger than they were before. Of course the betrayed husband or wife can trust their spouse again – many, many marriages have recovered from infidelity, and God's power to change the human heart is infinite.

But, at the same time, what's happened, whatever it is, can't be recalled. "O, call back yesterday, bid time return," says Shakespeare's tragic Richard II. We've all been there, wishing that something we've done could be undone, that words we've spoken could be unsaid.

Forgiveness doesn't always mean that we have to have a continuing relationship with someone who's harmed us. But sometimes it does. And so, somewhere in how we deal with what's been done to us, there has to be a way of acknowledging what's happened, but in the context of believing that they intend never to do it again.

This might mean that some things have to change. It might be on a purely practical level. Someone who's been convicted of fraud might have been forgiven by her victims. That doesn't mean that she's going to be appointed as the church treasurer. Someone who's had an affair might have been forgiven by his wife. But she'll always know that he's capable of it, and they'll need to work out ways in which he can be accountable to her. Forgiveness doesn't mean that the clock is set to zero. God can raise the dead, and God can raise dead marriages, dead friendships, and dead reputations. But sin changes things.

In John 20:27 the risen Jesus invites Thomas to put his fingers into his wounds. In Revelation 5:6, John sees "a Lamb, looking as if it had been slain, standing at the centre of the throne". Christ was raised with his scars, and so are we.

5. Forgiveness doesn't come with guarantees

Whatever forgiveness is, it isn't a transaction. We don't forgive someone in the expectation that they'll change and become a better person. It isn't really about the other person at all: it's about how we choose to deal with our own feelings of anger and hurt and our own desire for revenge. So, if they harm us again, or let us down, or harm someone else, that's sad. But it doesn't mean that we were wrong to forgive them, because forgiveness isn't a bargain. It's a gift.

Maybe our gift does change someone. Maybe it helps them become a better person in some way. Or maybe it doesn't. Acts 20:35 records Jesus' words, "It is more blessed to give than to receive." This makes psychological sense as well as spiritual. Being under an obligation to someone is hard, and there's no greater obligation than being forgiven. This is what lies behind the saying in Proverbs 25:21 – quoted by Paul in Romans 12:20 – "If your enemy is hungry, give him food to eat; if he is thirsty, give him water to drink. In doing this, you will heap burning coals on his head."

If we've been hurt, we can choose forgiveness as our Christian response. Then the person who's done the hurting is faced with a choice, too. Will they learn, repent, and change? Or will they be consumed with resentment and lash out in retaliation? But that's not our choice; it's theirs. Our choice is to forgive. Sometimes, as Mark Twain said, "Forgiveness is the fragrance that the violet sheds on the heel that has crushed it" – and that's all. But that fragrance is sweet.

So, then: after all this talk of what forgiveness is *not*, what can we say about what it is? And we have to begin by saying that it isn't just one thing, and it isn't quick or easy. But here's the first thing.

Forgiveness means **setting aside a desire for revenge**.

When we have been hurt, the instinct is to retaliate, or to wish the other person harm. Most of us are civilized and rational enough to feel a bit ashamed of this instinct, but it's there. We read about the betrayed wife who pours paint on her husband's prized car and think, "Good for you." Or we watch the action film where the bad guy dies in a hail of bullets and feel somehow satisfied: yes, that's how it's supposed to be. People ought to get what's coming to them.

Most of us don't take our desire for revenge as far as this. But we might try to wound another person by the words we use, to their face or behind their back. If it's a situation at work, we might scheme against them and try to do them harm. If we discover that things aren't going well for them – if they're ill or in pain – we'll be quietly glad about it.

Martin Luther King famously said in 1967, the year before his assassination: "The arc of the moral universe is long, but it bends toward justice." Something deep within us responds to that. We want to believe that, either in this world or the next, people who've done wrong will pay for it.

A criminal who has defrauded someone or stolen or committed violence needs to pay the penalty for the crime. Because society can't be safe and prosperous without a consistent and enforceable criminal justice system, the law cannot forgive. Sometimes this makes the law look harsh, or even ridiculous. As I write, a now former magistrate, Nigel Allcoat, is in the headlines because, forced to impose court charges on a destitute asylum seeker that he believed were unjust and stupid, he paid them out of his own pocket. He was suspended and told he would be investigated: the law is the law.

But a person can resolve to lay justice aside. Someone who's been hurt by what another person has done can decide that they will not seek revenge and they will not attempt to make the other person pay. They won't speak or work against them and they won't take pleasure in their misfortunes.

That can be a matter of psychological and moral self-preservation, especially when hurt goes deep and bitterness becomes embedded in our whole being. Someone has said that holding on to a grudge is like drinking poison and expecting the other person to die. Hatred is no good for us, even when the object of our hatred might richly deserve it. It makes us mean, it makes us sad, and it makes us ill. Forgiveness, at its most basic level, is saying: "I'm letting that go. I am no longer going to let myself be defined by what has been done to me. My life will not be shaped by another person's evil. How I live and how I feel will no longer take account of their sin against me."

This is enormously liberating. For Christians, it means a reorientation away from ourselves and how we feel – angry, disappointed, bewildered, resentful – towards God. A classic example of this is Corrie ten Boom. Arrested by the Nazis as a young woman in Holland for the crime of hiding Jews, she was sent with her sister, Betsie, to Ravensbrück concentration camp, where Betsie died in the appalling conditions. Throughout it all, Corrie maintained her Christian faith.

After the war she became an evangelist, later writing about her experiences in her book *The Hiding Place* (Hodder & Stoughton, 2004). On one occasion, in 1947, she was speaking at a meeting in Munich when she recognized one of the guards from the camp.

> *Now he was in front of me, hand thrust out: "A fine
> message, Fräulein! How good it is to know that, as
> you say, all our sins are at the bottom of the sea!"*

He didn't remember her, but she remembered him, and the
shame of walking naked past him with her sister. Her blood
froze and she couldn't take his hand. Her description of what
happened next is unforgettable.

> *It could not have been many seconds that he stood
> there, hand held out, but to me it seemed hours as
> I wrestled with the most difficult thing I had ever
> had to do. And still I stood there with the coldness
> clutching my heart. But forgiveness is not an
> emotion – I knew that too. Forgiveness is an act of
> the will, and the will can function regardless of the
> temperature of the heart.*
>
> *"Jesus, help me!" I prayed silently. "I can lift my
> hand. I can do that much. You supply the feeling."
> And so woodenly, mechanically, I thrust my hand
> into the one stretched out to me. And as I did, an
> incredible thing took place. The current started
> in my shoulder, raced down my arm, sprang into
> our joined hands. And then this healing warmth
> seemed to flood my whole being, bringing tears to
> my eyes. "I forgive you, brother!" I cried. "With all
> my heart!"*

Does the "feeling" of which Corrie wrote always accompany the
act of forgiveness? No. But she knew from her own experience
how important forgiveness was for healing. After the war, she

set up a home in Holland for victims of Nazi brutality. This is what she discovered: "Those who were able to forgive their former enemies were able also to return to the outside world and rebuild their lives, no matter what the physical scars. Those who nursed their bitterness remained invalids. It was as simple and as horrible as that."

Corrie was well taught. She got it absolutely right when she said that forgiveness was an act of will. But when she handed over the outcome to Jesus, she released a great spiritual energy, which turned a duty into a joy and a handshake into an embrace.

Her experience points towards the second characteristic of forgiveness: for Christians, forgiveness is **more than just moving on**. Resolving not to take or seek revenge is the key to forgiveness. But, with all the caveats and qualifications mentioned above – no, it won't necessarily make you feel better and you don't have to be best friends with the person who's injured you – Christians are called to something better than that.

It's not just about what we don't do. Christian discipleship is about coming to reflect in our own minds and hearts the mind and heart of God. God's orientation is towards grace. So along with setting revenge aside – and even setting justice aside – we're called to take another, even harder step. We are called to will the best for the other person.

If it weren't for the example of people like Corrie ten Boom, this could seem impossibly difficult. It is beyond many of us. We have perhaps been too deeply wounded. The other person shows no remorse. They have prospered and flourished, and we have not. We might, through gritted teeth, forgo revenge. But positively wishing them good, praying for their well-being, is too much.

And here we run into some uncomfortable words of Jesus. In Luke 6:32–36 (the thought is the same in the Sermon on the Mount in Matthew 5) he says: "If you love those who love you, what credit is that to you? Even sinners love those who love them. And if you do good to those who are good to you, what credit is that to you? Even sinners do that. And if you lend to those from whom you expect repayment, what credit is that to you? Even sinners lend to sinners, expecting to be repaid in full. But love your enemies, do good to them, and lend to them without expecting to get anything back. Then your reward will be great, and you will be children of the Most High, because he is kind to the ungrateful and wicked" (NIV). In other words, Christians are to be different.

For most of us, the memory of old injuries fades as time goes by. Time really does heal. We see things more clearly. Sometimes we might even be brought to understand that we bear some of the blame for what's gone wrong. This happens whether we're Christians or not. It's part of God's common grace to all human beings. We get over things and we move on.

But Christians are called to a different level of moral and spiritual effort altogether. We are indwelt by the Holy Spirit. We aren't just called to forgo revenge against our enemies; we're called to love them. It's this that so many of us find impossibly difficult. But we need to be clear about what love is. It's not a feeling – though we are human beings, not calculating machines, and everything we do and think involves feelings of some kind. Loving forgiveness is an intention. Resolving not to take revenge is at best neutral. Resolving to follow in the footsteps of Christ, who even when he was dying on the cross prayed that God would forgive those who had crucified him, involves a movement of the heart towards the other person.

Samuel Taylor Coleridge (1772–1834) was a great Christian thinker as well as a poet. In his best-known poem, *The Rime of the Ancient Mariner*, he offers an acute insight into the nature of grace. The Mariner is alone aboard a ship crewed by dead men and surrounded by loathsome water-snakes – "A thousand thousand slimy things/ Lived on, and so did I," he says. His soul is in agony. He cannot pray. But his spiritual paralysis ends when he sees the water-snakes not as loathsome but as lovely:

> *O happy living things! No tongue*
> *Their beauty might declare:*
> *A spring of love gushed from my heart,*
> *And I blessed them unaware:*
> *Sure my kind saint took pity on me,*
> *And I blessed them unaware.*

The Albatross, hung from his neck as a curse, falls into the sea and he can pray. Love begins when we stop seeing just the ugliness in other people and start to see their beauty too.

One man who has had to think about forgiveness more than most is Harvey Thomas. He was Margaret Thatcher's press adviser and was staying in the Grand Hotel in Brighton when it was bombed by the IRA in 1984. Five people were killed and thirty-four injured. The wife of Norman Tebbit, the Tory politician, was left disabled. Harvey fell through three floors of the hotel and was injured, but recovered.

Harvey is a larger-than-life character who worked with Billy Graham on his crusades and has a fund of good tales to tell about his days in politics. I interviewed him a few years ago when I became aware of his story. Because Harvey Thomas had written to the man convicted of planting the bomb while he was in prison, offering him forgiveness.

After Patrick Magee – described by the judge at his trial in 1986 as "a man of exceptional cruelty and inhumanity" – was released, he visited Harvey in his home and met his family. The two men have shared platforms and reflected on their experiences and attitudes. For Harvey, though, the process began earlier. Fourteen years after the bombing, in 1998, he was preaching in Louisville, Kentucky, at St Matthew's Baptist Church. "I was speaking on Matthew 6:12–15, where Jesus says 'If you forgive men when they sin against you, your heavenly father will also forgive you', and God spoke to my heart," he told me.

"As I was speaking, I was convicted – I was speaking on reconciliation, but I had not practised it. I said this from the pulpit – 'I am not practising this, so I will write to Patrick Magee and tell him that I forgive him.' I prayed with Marlies, my wife, and I wrote to him and said, 'As a Christian, I forgive you.'"

His forgiveness, he says, was unconditional, and he didn't expect a reply. But his letter set off a train of events that he could not have foreseen, and has led to deep insights and rich encounters. "Pat replied very graciously," said Thomas, "though he said, 'We would see the events of those times very differently.' I wrote back and said 'I'd love to meet you one day.'"

The correspondence lapsed until 2000, when all the Republican prisoners were released under the terms of the Good Friday Agreement. Not long after that, Thomas and Magee met for the first time through Anne Gallagher, founder of the Seeds of Hope reconciliation project.

"I met Pat MacGee at her home, and we talked for four or five hours," Harvey recalled. "He couldn't understand why I would forgive him. He explained his reasons. He said, 'You lose a bit of your soul every time someone is hurt because of what you do, but we were at war.' He still believes that at that time, they had exhausted every other means."

I asked Harvey what he thought forgiveness was, and I remember the pause as he thought. "It starts with respect," he said. "I had regarded him as a violent person and as a terrorist, until the Bible spoke to me and Jesus said 'Forgive.' And 1 Peter says, 'Honour all men, respect all people.' I found I had not got that respect for Pat, and for many others. I needed a biblical respect for individuals."

And so: "We were two people meeting and starting from scratch. I was and am interested in knowing who people are. We need to start from respect – not from tolerance. Tolerance is bad. It says, 'You're wrong, but I put up with that because I'm a nice person.' Tolerance is wrong – it's phoney, it's a cop-out. On this occasion, I was able to change my attitude. I would no longer look at Pat as the person who blew me up. I didn't condone what he did, or agree with it, or expect others to feel the same as me."

This insight came to mean a great deal to him. In his post-Brighton career, Thomas became involved with the charity African Enterprise. In that capacity he met people who had done terrible things, for instance in the Rwanda genocide. Was it, I asked him, possible to understand and value even them? He said: "My gut feeling is that if individuals lose their individuality – which is nearly always a cultural or emotional movement – then they can collectively get into that demonic, evil state. If you take each individual away from that, if you separate them from that culture, they will probably revert to being a normal human being."

So perhaps respect becomes an attempt to find and bless God for what's still human in someone who's done even the most terrible things, while standing resolutely against what they have done – and doing it, as Harvey said, unconditionally, with no expectation of any return.

I found his story deeply moving and deeply challenging. I believe, now, that it has a place in how we understand the whole arc and process of forgiveness.

Perhaps forgiveness might begin with letting go, resolving not to take revenge. It might move on to a sense of respect and a quest for points of contact even with those who have hurt us most. It might, in time, move on to a deep and fully godly love, of the kind that Jesus showed Peter when they shared breakfast on the beach after his resurrection, and which he would have shown Judas too.

But no one has the right to tell another person where they should be at any given moment. Forgiveness, at whatever level, has to be free, or it isn't real.

Love is a process and a gift. It can't be compelled – pastors who tell their people that they ought to forgive and love their enemies aren't helping them; they're abusing them. Love is one of the fruits of the Spirit (Galatians 5:22). Fruit grows at its own speed, and the task of the gardener is to make sure that it's given the right conditions to grow well, protected from what might harm it. The fruits of the Spirit grow at their own speed too, and the pastor's task is just the same.

I think we make forgiveness too easy. It isn't easy at all. It goes to the roots of our identity, our relationships, our sense of self-worth, and what we most value – and that's before we even start thinking about our faith. But, as well as a calling, it's a gift from God. Honest, open-eyed forgiveness can liberate and bless.

6

Spiritual growth: How the church gets in the way

A friend of mine hasn't decorated her kitchen for years. One reason, I suspect, is that lovingly preserved on one wall are the pencil marks that chart the growth of her son, from when he was about three feet nothing until he could rest his chin on her head. That's how growth happens – upwards. It's linear. It's the same intellectually, too. We get through our schooldays and sit our exams. Perhaps we go to college or university. We acquire qualifications through accumulating knowledge. We're growing because we're amassing data.

The danger is that we import those ideas into the church when really we ought to leave them at the door. We risk buying in to a fundamentally secular idea of spiritual growth, which cramps and limits disciples of Jesus when we should be setting them free.

Search online for "Spiritual Growth" and you'll find literally thousands of pages. Not all of them are Christian by any means.

But what many Christian websites, books, sermons, and programmes have in common is that they use the language of teaching. Discipleship is about studying the Bible, learning more about Christian doctrine, what the different books say, and how it all fits together. Or it's about how to evangelize, perhaps – what we might say to someone who's interested in our faith. Perhaps we want to know what the Bible says about ethical matters such as divorce or homosexuality or the environment. Or maybe it's about prayer – how can we do it more and better?

There's nothing wrong with learning stuff. I make my living writing books and articles I hope people will want to read. I want them to learn and I want them to think. But I try not to imagine that I'm doing very much towards helping them grow. What if Christian growth isn't about learning more, even if it's learning more about the Bible? What if it doesn't have much to do with church, even? What if Christian growth, as a category all of its own, doesn't really exist?

A few years ago I was the minister of a small church in the Midlands. It kept on surprising me by making a success of things I never thought would work. One of these was a mid-week afternoon Bible-study group. Around eight or a dozen of us met once a week, mainly women and mainly a good deal older than me.

I'm embarrassed to think of the years of theological education I'd accumulated by then – think two university degrees, plus time at theological college. But I look back at those meetings and I don't think of what I might have taught, but of what I learned. Those were incredibly rich gatherings, because of the years of experience and reflection those women brought to them. Again and again I'd leave with my mind full of what I'd been shown and thinking "I must preach that".

These were mainly mature Christian people, some of them with a deep knowledge of the Bible. But their maturity wasn't measured by the quantity of knowledge that they'd gathered – I was ahead of them there – but by its quality. There was a texture about their faith, which had nothing to do with how much they knew, and everything to do with how it had helped to shape them into the people they were. The mature Christian isn't someone who can reel off a verse for every occasion and who knows exactly when to pull you up because what you've said isn't doctrinally "sound". The mature Christian is someone who has lived fully and richly, and brought every part of his or her life into the presence of Christ and under his authority.

What that Bible-study group taught me is that Christian maturity isn't something separate from the development of our whole personhood, as though we can grow as Christians without growing as people. Growth is multifaceted, many-layered and multidirectional – and, far from it happening through church and church-based activities, these can actually hinder it.

One of the greatest of the early Church Fathers, the second-century bishop Irenaeus, is often quoted as writing this: "The glory of God is a human being fully alive." He didn't say exactly that, but he came close enough – and the insight itself is a profound one. Human beings are the most complex, wonderful, and terrible creatures on earth. There's not much in the way of DNA that separates us from our nearest relative, the chimpanzee, but what we've done with it makes all the difference in the world. In our intelligence, imagination, and creativity, we are as far ahead of even the most intelligent animals as they are ahead of an amoeba.

That intellectual capacity doesn't necessarily come with an equivalent moral capacity, and often the ones who suffer because of that are those same animals. And we're increasingly recognizing, too, that animals are capable of far more intelligent behaviour than we ever imagined. But our minds contain layer upon layer of thought and emotion. We can think, and think about what we thought. We can dream – and, most importantly of all, we can create. And, as far as we know, human beings represent the only life of this kind in the universe.

So perhaps what Irenaeus meant was this. It's in human beings, set free to flourish and be all that they can be, fulfilled in relationships with one another and in satisfying work, living as spiritual beings in the light of eternity, that the nature of God is most fully seen and known. We're amazed by the created universe, struck dumb by the glory revealed by the amazing pictures of galaxies and nebulae sent back by the Hubble space telescope. But what should really astonish us is the glorious complexity and potential of the person standing next to us in the supermarket queue.

In all of history there's only been one person of whom Irenaeus' words are really true. Jesus was the "human being fully alive" who truly showed us the glory of God. And Jesus said: "I have come that they may have life, and have it to the full" (John 10:10, NIV). His desire for his disciples was that they should be as glorious as he was. This is the thought behind Paul's words when he says: "For God, who said, 'Let light shine out of darkness,' made his light shine in our hearts to give us the light of the knowledge of God's glory displayed in the face of Christ" (2 Corinthians 4:6). The power and glory of the act of creation is matched and surpassed by the power and glory of the act of re-creation, in which human beings are transformed by the knowledge of God's glory in the face of Christ.

Irenaeus also said that Christ "became what we are in order to make us what he is". Another of the Church Fathers, the fourth-century bishop Athanasius, put it even more strongly: "God has become man so that man might become God."

So the witness of the Bible and the earliest church to what God wants to do in our lives is clear. He wants us to live the fullest and richest lives of which we're capable. He has created a vast, complex, exciting, and fascinating world, full of possibilities and potential. It's as we engage with this world, exploring it and enjoying it, that we're enabled to reflect more and more of God's own creativity. The more we learn, grow, and change, the more we shine out his glory.

The risk is that we become so fixated on the things that happen in church that we end up with misshapen disciples whose horizons have been narrowed by the gospel rather than broadened by it.

Churches can be all-absorbing, taking over our spare time, becoming the focus of our social life, and taxing our emotions and energy – not to mention our bank accounts. Somewhere along the line, a lot of churches have performed a sort of quantum leap into a parallel universe: people support meetings, instead of meetings supporting people. In a praiseworthy and sincere desire to build people up and keep them to their profession, we can create zones of spiritual sterility in which non-conventional ideas and behaviour are excluded. Songs are about me and how I feel. Prayers are about how we get on together. Meetings focus on buildings, organization, and finance.

Now, I believe in church. Church stops me from being selfish – or at least, quite so selfish. In the normal way of things, I can choose my own company, decide what I want to do and when I want to do it, and generally go my own way. Being part of a church means I accept I have responsibilities. I don't want to go to a meeting, but I go anyway. I'm a traditionally reserved Englishman who'd really rather not talk to anyone at all unless it's an absolute emergency, but when I go to church and see someone who's on their own, I have to. Church makes me a better person.

Church expands my mind and spirit. In middle age I find I've accumulated a good many opinions. But these can very easily ossify into prejudice. The risk is that we read only the work of people who think like us and talk only to people who agree with us. It's nice and safe. But when I go to church I hear things I hadn't thought of before and I realize that people really do think very differently from me. I learn a lot and sometimes I change my mind.

Most of all, church makes me pay attention to God. Do I always enjoy the worship? No. Sometimes the songs are irritating or I can't concentrate on the sermon or there are too many toddlers who don't seem to appreciate the glories of eighteenth-century English hymnody (I know, it's strange). But for an hour and a half on Sunday morning, I have no excuse for thinking about anything other than God.

But church isn't everything. Paul wrote to the Corinthians: "We all, who with unveiled faces contemplate the Lord's glory, are being transformed into his image with ever-increasing glory, which comes from the Lord, who is the Spirit" (2 Corinthians 3:18). That doesn't just happen in church. It happens in the world. There's a hymn that begins: "Here from the world we turn, Jesus to seek." It's lovely, but it always grates a little. I find myself wanting to sing, "Here *to* the world we turn, Jesus to seek."

So maybe there are some churches that ought to be asking a little less of their congregations, so that they can ask a lot more. Fewer meetings, less pressure to attend and conform, more affirmation of what has, on the face of it, nothing to do with church at all. Because growth is not just linear: the whole person grows.

Think back to the child at the beginning of this chapter, whose growth is marked by marks on the kitchen wall. The physical changes are what's visible. But the other changes are far more significant. There's a growth in mental sophistication, emotional complexity, empathy, judgment, and skills. The journey from childhood to adulthood is about far more than an increase in physical stature. And it is made possible not just by the passage of time, but by how we respond to the challenges of new experiences and insights that test us and develop our mental and spiritual muscles.

I grow when I wrestle with a problem at work for hours or days and end up solving it. Maybe I've called in colleagues to help; maybe I've had to learn new skills or drawn on new resources. I grow when I've had a conversation with someone I've never talked to before. We've found shared interests. I've decided I like this person and a relationship begins.

I grow when I've made myself go out for a run on a cold, damp afternoon when I'd rather be indoors. It might be pathetically slow, but I've pushed my limits again. I grow when I've read a book or watched a film that's forced me to see the world through someone else's eyes. I've found myself understanding someone's life instead of judging it.

I grow when I've spent time with someone who needs me – a child, a parent, a stranger. It's made me put someone else first. I grow when I've needed someone else. It's taught me to be dependent and challenged my pride and self-reliance. I grow when I've experienced beauty. I grow when I've experienced love, grief, and pain.

These are the kinds of things that can happen in a church context. But most of the time they don't. Church focuses on church things: prayer, the Bible, worship. And that's fine, but only if we understand that church is there to nourish our growth and integrate it with gospel truth. It's not there to draw lines round it, as though God is only interested in certain activities. Every part of our lives belongs to him.

It's when we've lived richly, thought deeply, and prayed intensely that we bring most glory to God, because it's then that we are most fully alive. Churches that take this seriously won't always enjoy the experience. It means setting people free from expectations and trusting them to follow Christ in their own way.

For instance: my own church tradition places a lot of value on being there – turning up to services. I do too – I think it's a good discipline and it's too easy to let things slide. But I recently spoke to a friend who'd had an encounter with a *Big Issue* seller. Probably, for most of us, if we pass someone selling that magazine, there are two options: buy it, or don't. She chose a third option and simply asked him how he was. He told her. He wasn't doing very well.

My friend couldn't do much, but she was moved by the story. It made her think about making a radical change in her discipleship. Maybe, instead of going to church every Sunday morning, she'd worship in a different way. She'd go and talk to homeless people and offer them what she could. For that hour she'd be available, for a cup of coffee or a sandwich, a listening ear, a prayer – whatever they needed. It would be a hour, because there'd have to be boundaries, but it would be something.

I've no idea if she'll do it. But, if she does, perhaps her church might see it as a mistake. Perhaps they'll think they've failed in not being attractive enough to keep her in the congregation. But I think she might grow, far more than she would even under the most godly and dynamic ministry imaginable.

There's a story in Luke's Gospel that most of us know by heart – so well, in fact, that we probably don't think there's much to learn from it any more. The parable of the Good Samaritan (Luke 10:25–37) tells us that we should be kind to other people and that, though someone might be a stranger or even an enemy, we should take the risk of helping them.

Only it's not quite like that. We might want to think of retitling the parable of the Good Samaritan "the parable of the priest and the Levite". The story tells of how the man going down from Jerusalem to Jericho was beaten up by robbers and left for dead. The priest and the Levite both pass by on the other side of the road and leave him there. But why?

The answer Jesus' hearers would have known instinctively is that he might have been dead – and, if they had touched a dead body, they would be ritually unclean. According to Numbers 19:16, "Anyone out in the open who touches someone who has been killed with a sword or someone who has died a natural death, or anyone who touches a human bone or a grave, will be unclean for seven days."

In other words, their desire to observe the letter of the law had overruled their compassion for someone who desperately needed help. The religion that should have warmed their hearts and opened their minds had turned them into people whose idea of what was right had been corrupted. Jesus takes the Samaritan, a hereditary enemy of the Jews who treated the victim with great generosity, as an example of what grace and mercy look like. "Go and do likewise," he said. It was the Samaritan, not the priest or the Levite, whose faith was mature

– who was the human being fully alive who showed the glory of God.

Sometimes our religion gets in the way, too. It narrows our understanding of grace. It doesn't nourish our growth; it stunts it. That story tells me that God isn't too worried about respectability. I think he quite likes it if we break the rules, as long as we do it for the right reasons. I don't think he'd mind if my friend took to skipping church on Sunday mornings to talk to homeless people. I think that God wants us to be open to the wonderful world that his loving creativity has given us. I think he wants us to seize every opportunity we can to live as fully and as generously as we can.

That's not always easy. We like rules and limits, and that's all right. But think back to Genesis, and one of God's first appearances in the Bible. He is a gardener, cutting back the thorns and thickets, making clearings, lawns, and pools, planting fruit trees. But I doubt if we're meant to imagine Eden as a show garden with not a leaf out of place. I don't think that's how he works.

We can be tempted to tame our wildernesses too much, in every sense. Order is good, but if our homes, our gardens, our countryside, or our theologies become too orderly, they become sterile. There's no room for surprise, for the unexpected or the challenging. Birds and animals need the undergrowth, the piles of leaves, the fallen tree that isn't hauled away. So do all of us; these things provide us with the things we don't know we need.

The Christian poet Gerard Manley Hopkins wrote: "What would the world be, once bereft/ Of wet and wildness? Let them be left,/ O let them be left, wildness and wet;/ Long live the weeds and the wilderness yet."

When churches try to make our lives too tidy, they don't help us grow. We need space to flourish according to our natures, among the weeds and the wilderness of the world outside the church walls.

7

Prayer is about God, not about us

Prayer is what Christians do. We do it in church on Sundays and we're supposed to do it at home. We probably have special meetings to do it during the week. Some years ago a Billy Graham evangelistic campaign introduced the idea of "prayer triplets" – groups of three who would covenant to meet together and pray for each other or for a particular cause. It caught on and it's still common. Christians pray.

I believe in prayer. Prayer is great. It's part of the glue that holds a congregation together. It connects us to God. It's biblical. It's natural. There are all sorts of prayers. The format many of us will have been taught is based on the ACTS acronym: Adoration, Confession, Thanksgiving, and Supplication. That works for me.

When congregations pray, it can be wonderful. The church I attend is small enough for us to be able to pray openly during services. That can be lovely, as people express what's on their hearts, in praise or petition. When people pray in small groups it can be an intense, intimate experience in which God is vividly present. Something happens; the combination of tension and peace is almost impossible to explain to someone who hasn't experienced it. When individuals pray, they can feel profoundly moved. Some feel guilt, as God shows them something in their life that shouldn't be there. Some feel sadness, or joy, or peace. There might be new spiritual insights, connections made for the first time.

But there are no guarantees. Sometimes congregational prayer is awkward, and you have the sense that someone's praying to fill a silence. Sometimes no one does, and that's even worse. Sometimes group prayer is dull and flat; no one has anything to say, and what they do say doesn't carry conviction. Sometimes individual prayer is boring or routine, and we wonder why we bother. Prayer is tricky. It needs to be learned.

I wonder if how evangelicals talk about prayer always matches up with what we actually do. Take daily prayer. It tends to be assumed that daily "quiet times" of prayer and Bible reading are the norm. In fact, for many of us they aren't. An Evangelical Alliance report in 2014 entitled *Time for Discipleship?* found that only 31 per cent said they set aside a substantial period of time each day to pray, with a further 32 per cent saying they tried to find a few minutes every day.

What's more, the research found that "[o]lder people (those born before 1960) are significantly more disciplined and structured in their prayer patterns". So the trend, as far as we can tell, is running against daily prayer – though some of those who are not very disciplined at the moment might become so in later life. Some might say that's a terrible indictment of our prayer life. I don't think so; I understand the value of daily time with God, but I'd like to hear pastors say loudly and clearly: "If that doesn't work for you, don't feel guilty."

I have reservations about the mood of prayer that seems to be encouraged, too. I won't name them, but some "prayer ministries" seem to infantilize our relationship with God in an unhelpful and unscriptural way. It's all about how we feel toward our heavenly Father. The problem here lies in imagining that fathers in the first century had exactly the same relationship with their children as fathers in the twenty-first. They did not, and far too much of the language about prayer that appears in our worship songs is unhistorical and unbiblical.

The disciples said to Jesus: "Lord, teach us to pray, just as John taught his disciples" (Luke 11:1). His answer was to teach them what we know as the Lord's Prayer. It's calm, structured, and simple but full of theology. You can say it without feeling very much at all, but it is "the prayer Jesus taught us to say". I'd like to hear pastors say, "It's OK to pray using other people's words. You can praise God using a psalm or you can praise him using 1662 English if that works for you. Your prayers of adoration are not about you and whether you've got the gift of the gab. They're about him."

Most of all, I wonder whether we've really thought through what we believe about our prayers of intercession. Prayers "for things" – "supplication" in the ACTS acronym – are some of the most natural of all. Jesus implied this himself. In the Sermon on the Mount he says: "Which of you if his son asks for bread, will give him a stone? Or if he asks for a fish, will give him a snake? If you, then, though you are evil, know how to give good gifts to your children, how much more will your Father in heaven give good gifts to those who ask him!" (Matthew 7:9–11, NIV).

We pray for things we need, when someone's ill, or we're worried about the future, or there are huge national or international problems that we're exposed to through TV or the internet. We ask God to help us and to change things. But I wonder how honest we are, with ourselves and with each other. I wonder how often we think about the limitations of intercessory prayer and about the responsibilities that the act of praying creates for us.

We've probably all asked questions at one time or another about how it works. Perhaps we've heard prayers for fine weather for the church picnic and thought, "Really? Will God adjust the path of the jet stream for us?" And what about everyone who's really hoping for a bit of rain on their allotment? Or there's the super-spiritual person who regularly prays for a parking space and finds that God never lets her down. We aren't sure how that works, either – does God just mark it with a sort of spiritual bollard?

But these examples are on the fringe of our worries about prayer. There are plenty of others that are more serious. Week by week we pray for peace, in Iraq or Afghanistan, Syria, or Sudan. Things just get worse. Or it comes very close to home: a spouse or a child is ill or in pain. We pray for them to get better and they don't. Healing is perhaps the most intractable of all these problems. The Bible is full of it; it's an article of faith for many churches that God heals, and we really want to believe it, but the verifiable medical evidence that it happens in real life is painfully thin.

At the same time, it's such a powerful instinct that we cannot *not* pray.

In the eighteenth century the idea grew up that God had set the world going and left it to its own devices, like a watchmaker who makes a watch, winds it up, and sets it going. Once it's started, it can't do anything else but tell the time. This idea was called "deism". Deists weren't atheists. They believed that there was a God; just that he wasn't all that relevant. His involvement with the world was limited to setting it going. So there was no point in asking God to change things; it just wasn't what he did.

That's a long way away from traditional Christian belief. Christians have always held that God is still involved with his creation. Jesus told us to ask, and we ask. But there's still that nagging question: can God really change things, or is that breaking his own rules?

One of the most helpful books about this I've read is by David Wilkinson, the principal of St John's College, Durham, and in a former life an astrophysicist. That's not irrelevant, because science is based on the idea that you can explain the world. It's ordered and orderly. But if God can overturn the rules of the world he's made, there's a problem. If he can and he chooses not to, there's another problem – and Wilkinson has experienced this in his own life as his wife, Alison, a Methodist minister, suffers from painful and debilitating rheumatoid arthritis.

In his 2015 book *When I Pray, What Does God Do?*, he's honest about his own struggles with prayer and has a refreshing chapter on the "everyday myths" that we ought to beware of. He also talks about the idea that prayer is just about changing the person who prays, rather than expecting God to do anything. It's this view that stems from the notion that miracles, in which God intervenes in the world to break the natural laws that he has created, are just impossible. The world runs like a clock, as those eighteenth-century deists believed, and there are no good reasons for expecting God to correct the mechanism through miracles.

Wilkinson cites influential philosophers such as Voltaire, Spinoza, and Hume, whose scepticism led to a "de-miraclizing" of the New Testament.

So, for example, the "miracle" of the loaves and fishes was really a miracle of sharing, because the example of the little boy who brought Jesus his food inspired others to do the same. And Jesus didn't really walk on water; it was just a sandbank, and the disciples were a bit confused.

Wilkinson says that the problem with this view is that it's based on out-of-date science – a mechanistic, Newtonian view of the world in which cause and effect can be plotted exactly. But we now know that the world doesn't operate like that at all. Quantum theory tells us that the small-scale structure of the world is, in the words of Christian physicist John Polkinghorne, "radically random": "By that he means it is unpredictable and nothing like a mechanical clock," says Wilkinson. "It is a world that is unpicturable, uncertain, and in which the cause of events cannot be fully specified."

So, suggests Wilkinson, there's plenty of room for God to act, because the system isn't closed at all. He can "push" electrons here and there and alter the course of events in the world without breaking any of the laws of nature. The problem is that too many theologians simply don't know enough about physics and are stuck with out-of-date science. Quantum theory doesn't answer all our questions, Wilkinson says cautiously, but it "may be one dimension of how God works in the world".

He also writes about "chaos theory". Again, this undermines Newton's idea that the world is predictable. It says that most systems in the world – for instance the weather – are very sensitive to change, so that a small disturbance will make them act very differently. Effectively that means they're unpredictable, a principle known as the "butterfly effect" after meteorologist Edward Lorenz, who asked in 1979, "Does the flap of a butterfly's wings in Brazil set off a tornado in Texas?"

But could we predict systems if we had a big-enough computer? No, says Wilkinson. In a fascinating illustration, he suggests a thought experiment in which a cue ball is struck against the rest of the snooker balls. Predicting where, in the absence of friction, they would all end up after one minute should be simple enough. But actually the system is chaotic. To predict their positions accurately we'd need to take into account effects as small as the gravitational attraction of an electron on the very edge of our galaxy – and a computer bigger than the universe.

This means that, at the macro level as well as the micro, the idea that the world is fixed and predictable is just wrong, and that arguments against an interventionist God don't work. So, Wilkinson says, chaos might give "space for God to work in unusual and specific ways within the scientific description of the world". Again he quotes John Polkinghorne, who says that chaos means that the world is open to the future: "This means that we can pray and God responds by working in the openness of a chaotic system." His own view is that claiming that science rules out miracles is folly.

Probably for most of us it's enough that God is a heavenly Father, and we don't worry too much about the mechanics of answered prayer. But if we don't understand how prayers of intercession work at a spiritual level, we can get prayer really wrong.

1. We can trivialize prayer

In his letter to the Philippians, Paul tells them: "[I]n every situation, by prayer and petition, with thanksgiving, present your requests to God." It's sometimes translated as "Pray about everything". Some do. Every situation is brought before God

– such as finding a parking space. Every decision that's not immediately clear is laid before him, with a request that he sort it out. God, after all, is sovereign. God can take charge of our life and show us what's best for us.

Of course. But a good rule for reading the Bible is always to remind ourselves that a text without a context is a pretext. And this context is anxiety. The sentence is introduced with "Do not be anxious about anything", and it's followed by "And the peace of God, which transcends all understanding, will guard your hearts and your minds in Christ Jesus" (Philippians 4:6–7).

In other words: when we are anxious we should pray and God will hear us. It's like a child who's frightened of the dark – his parent will run up the stairs and comfort him. And sometimes, because the world is the way it is, the dark will contain real monsters and the child will need defending – and the parent is there. But children grow up. If we are Christians with any degree of maturity, we'll have learned how to cope with the bad stuff. We'll have developed the right reactions and the right Christlike character to be able to do the right thing and take responsibility for our own behaviour.

When we ask God for something, we're saying: "We want the world to be other than it is, because we'd prefer it that way, for ourselves or for other people."

When our prayers are for others, they're more likely to be honest and good. Our hearts go out to people who are in need and we want their anxieties and pain to stop. When they're for ourselves, we need to be careful. We're asking God to change the world for us.

Sometimes, perhaps, we need to cultivate an acceptance of the present moment, with its discomforts and irritations, and not be so needy. Part of growing up is learning to live with disappointment and frustration, and realizing that it's OK not to have everything we want.

2. We can abuse prayer

Sometimes it's glaringly obvious – to most people, anyway – that this is happening. There are preachers who teach a "prosperity gospel", namely that God wants all his people to be rich. This teaching tends to flourish when there's a lot of inequality in society and when a lot of money is being made by a few people. So these preachers find a hearing in developing countries, in rising Asian countries, and in the US, which has always valued success. One of them, US-based Creflo Dollar – and, yes, that's his real name – hit the headlines recently when he asked his followers to donate $65 million for a new, top-of-the-range private jet. In a tweet that was hastily deleted but widely shared, he wrote: "Jesus bled and died for us so that we can lay claim to the promise of financial prosperity."

We shouldn't underestimate the fear that not having enough money can generate in people. It's not wrong to want enough, and to pray for that. But these people prostitute prayer. They think it's a means to an end – and the end is just more money. There are other ways of abusing prayer that perhaps aren't so obvious. Often teachers on prayer encourage us to be specific in what we ask for. In one of his sermons on prayer ("Order and Argument in Prayer"), the great nineteenth-century Baptist preacher C. H. Spurgeon wrote: "It seems to me that prayer should be distinct, the asking for something definitely and distinctly because the mind has realized its distinct need of such a thing, and therefore must plead for it. It is well not to beat around the bush in prayer, but to come directly to the point."

No one argues with Spurgeon. But the danger in being too specific in our prayers is that we end up telling God what we want, rather than letting him tell us what we need. Prayers can sound as though we're giving God orders. At their worst, this kind of prayer can be used as a weapon. Someone who prays that her minister will be given the gift of preaching more interesting sermons probably has an agenda of her own.

But those agendas easily creep into our prayers. If there's something we feel passionately about – maybe a huge moral question such as abortion or euthanasia – it's easy to assume that God's on our side. When we feel deeply about an issue like poverty, it's easy to assume that the government in power isn't trying to do anything about it, or that what they're doing is wrong, and that it's because they don't care. So it's easy to find ourselves praying that they'll see things our way.

But Spurgeon was right to point out the danger from the other side: that we pray so generally that we ask for nothing at all. There's nothing wrong with believing passionately in a cause and praying for God's blessing upon it. But the more strongly we feel, the more responsibility we have. Along with that commitment has to go humility and self-knowledge. We need the grace to acknowledge that we might be wrong and that someone else's opinion is worth listening to.

In the book of Joshua, there's a strange story of his meeting with what we take to be an angel.

"Now when Joshua was near Jericho, he looked up and saw a man standing in front of him with a drawn sword in his hand. Joshua went up to him and asked, 'Are you for us or for our enemies?' 'Neither,' he replied, 'but as commander of the army of the Lord I have now come'" (5:13–14).

In other words: we don't co-opt God into fighting our battles for us, no matter how worthy the cause seems. God is free. We abuse prayer when we try to use it to preach our own opinions.

3. We can mechanize prayer

Another Spurgeon story: five young students were spending a Sunday in London, so they went to hear the famed Mr Spurgeon preach. While they waited for the doors of the Metropolitan Tabernacle to open, a stout, bearded man offered to show them round: "Would you like to see the church's boiler room?" Out of politeness, they agreed. He took them down a stairway and quietly opened a door. On the other side was a room with around 700 people praying inside. "This is our boiler room," he said quietly, before introducing himself: it was Spurgeon, of course.

It's a great story and it's inspired an international "Boiler Room" prayer network. The idea is that what happens in the church service is powered by what happens in the prayer meeting. I really question that. I think that what happens in the church service is powered by God.

I believe that God is free to do what he likes. If he chooses to pour out revival on a congregation after 700 people in a basement have prayed for it, he will. If he chooses to do it when it's just one, and she isn't too sure about the whole business, he will. Not every miracle in the Bible required great faith. Sometimes Jesus helped people whose faith was minimal. The father of a demonized boy said to Jesus: "I believe; help my unbelief!" (Mark 9:24, ESV). No one at all believed he could raise Lazarus (John 11).

Is there no connection between prayer and God's action? Of course there is. When Jesus was rejected at Nazareth, Matthew tells us that he "did not do many miracles there because of their lack of faith" (13:58, NIV). Mark puts it even more strongly: "He could not do any miracles there, except lay his hands on a few people who were ill and heal them" (6:5). But there's no *necessary* connection.

God is not moved by the numbers of people praying. He is not more likely to answer prayers if we gather for prayer at five in the morning, either, or if we go without food while we're praying. That's not how it works. That's what the priests of Baal thought when they danced around his altar and cut themselves in an effort to persuade him to light the sacrificial fire (1 Kings 18:25–29). Elijah knew that God would send the fire in his own good time.

It isn't what we choose to do that matters. It's what God chooses to do. It's all too easy for us to imagine prayer as our side of a bargain, requiring a response from him. But we cannot bribe God or coerce him. The biblical writers were aware of this. They lived in a world in which an elaborate system of sacrifice and religious observance was used to express and regulate the relationship between God and human beings. But they always knew that their sacrifices weren't the main thing.

The psalmist says: "Sacrifice and offering you did not desire, but my ears you have opened" (40:6). The reference is to a servant who is offered his freedom but chooses to stay with his master; the master will "take him to the door or the door-post and pierce his ear with an awl" (Exodus 21:6).

Prayer can be the equivalent of sacrifices and burnt offerings. It's good, but we should never imagine that it binds God in any way. Far more important is the deep-down relationship of trust and commitment. Our ears have been pierced; we are marked as his, whether he answers our prayers or not. Does this mean that our prayer meetings are pointless? Of course not. Enormous spiritual energies are released and channelled when Christians pray. It's entirely right to do so. When we pray, if we pray as we ought, we are not just asking God to change external realities. We are listening to him and offering ourselves to him.

A great psalm of repentance says this: "You do not delight in sacrifice, or I would bring it; you do not take pleasure in burnt offerings. My sacrifice, O God, is a broken spirit; a broken and contrite heart, you, God, will not despise" (Psalm 51:16–17). What God chooses to do in response to our prayers is up to him. What he wants to see in the one who prays is the broken and contrite heart.

The novelist Jon McGregor's first book, *If Nobody Speaks of Remarkable Things* (Bloomsbury, 2002), is the story of a summer's day on an inner-city street. McGregor is a Christian. The book is extraordinarily beautiful. At its heart is a moment of terrible drama and a single sentence: a character "wakes gently, lifted through a gap in the way of things".

We know all about the way of things. The way of things is the inexorable succession of cause and effect, the clock ticking on just as its maker intended. It's Newtonian physics: if you know the angle at which the cue ball hits the black, you know where the black will go. There are no miracles. Jesus walked on a sandbank, not on the water. If the cells of your body divide too fast you have cancer and you will die; if your husband commits adultery the marriage is over; if this man has a gun he will use it to kill. It's the way of things. When we pray, we believe that God can lift us through a gap in the way of things. It doesn't have to be the way everyone thinks it does, because God is free.

Another novelist, Frederick Buechner, wrote about a medieval monk, Godric of Finchale (c. 1065–1170). In one section of *Godric*, he talks about prayer. It is, he says, "shooting shafts into the dark. What mark they strike, if any, who's to say? It's reaching for a hand you cannot touch. The silence is so fathomless that prayers like plummets vanish into the sea. You beg. You whimper. You load God down with empty praise. You tell him sins that he already knows full well. You seek to change his changeless will. Yet Godric prays the way he breathes, for else his heart would wither in his breast. Prayer is the wind that fills his sail."

And just sometimes, "by God's grace, a prayer is heard".

8

How good teaching is killing good preaching

In most evangelical churches it's the sermon, rather than the Eucharist or Communion, that is at the heart of the service. That's why the traditional Nonconformist church has a huge pulpit in the middle with the Communion table underneath it. It's making a statement: this is what counts. In old Welsh chapels the elected deacons used to sit in a special pew at the front, the *sedd fawr*. Among other things, it was a sign that they were the guardians of the minister's orthodoxy. Sermons mattered and truth mattered.

Today the church building is likely to be dominated by a music group, and that says something about what we value too. But still today, in their preparation time, ministers are likely to spend far longer on the sermon than on any other part of the service. And evangelical churches are still passionate about biblical truth. One of evangelicalism's defining characteristics is its concern for right doctrine, leading to right living. What does the Bible say? What does it mean? And what does it mean to me?

In my own Baptist tradition everything before the sermon used to be known as the "preliminaries". Nowadays – absurdly – everything before the sermon is likely to be called the "worship" time (as though we can't worship God by listening). But there's still the sense that it's when we come to the sermon that we've arrived at what the service is really about, because that's when the teaching begins.

I want to honour that desire to engage with the Bible. I value the sense of expectancy and hunger that's there when a congregation believes that divine truth is going to be spoken from a human mouth. I believe in preaching. But let's not call it teaching. They are different animals, requiring different gifts and techniques. Of course, they shade into each other: some preaching will teach and some teaching will preach. But they are not the same.

I believe we sell preaching short when we call it teaching. I think it's the wrong way of understanding what goes on in those Sunday services. I think it deadens the act of preaching. It encourages us to think of it as the transmission of information. It's much more than that.

The English word "preach" comes from a Latin word meaning "proclaim", which translates the Greek word "*kerusso*" in the Gospels. Actually in older translations "preach" is used to translate various Greek words, including words meaning "proclaim", "announce", and "announce good news". But the word *kerusso* means "proclaim as a herald". It's what John the Baptist did in the wilderness (Matthew 3:1). Jesus told his disciples to "preach this message: 'The kingdom of heaven is near'" (Matthew 10:7, NET Bible). Paul wrote, "Jews demand signs and Greeks look for wisdom, but we preach Christ crucified" (1 Corinthians 1:22–23, NIV).

Of course, the New Testament talks about teaching as well. The word for "teaching", *didasko*, is used nearly 100 times – and no one is saying that we can do without it. We need to know what the Bible says. We need to understand the key doctrines of our faith. We need to know how to live, shining like stars in a dark world as we "hold out the word of life" (Philippians 2:15). Our faith has a content, and patiently learning that content is part of our discipleship. But I don't believe that the pulpit, or the lectern, or the platform, is a very good place for teaching. I believe that if preachers approach their congregations with the intention of imparting information, they will probably fail. If they succeed, the congregation will probably forget.

Teaching is part of a pastor's role. But sermons are a really bad way of doing that. In recent years researchers have studied the different ways in which people learn intensively. We know that one of the best ways of learning is through doing. We know that some people just hate being sat down and talked at. Discussion is good – lots of people learn through being really engaged with other people, arguing and bouncing ideas off them. People learn visually, through being able to see pictures that translate abstract concepts – or by creating their own art. Games are good. Having people learn through presenting their own take on an issue is brilliant. Making them sit still and listen for twenty-five minutes, probably without even taking notes? That probably ranks as just about the worst teaching method imaginable.

Now, actually, in most churches these other teaching methods *are* used – some of them, at least. But they're used in home groups or mid-week study groups – and these are where the really valuable teaching takes place, as people can interact and question, and go at their own pace. Does this mean that sermons are pointless? No. But we don't listen to sermons primarily to be taught stuff, whether it's biblical history, doctrine, or life application. Sermons are better than that.

There's a reason why what ministers do in churches Sunday by Sunday is usually called preaching – *kerusso*, proclaiming – rather than teaching. Preaching is what happens when you announce two life-changing, world-shaking truths: that the kingdom of God has come and that Jesus is Lord. It is what one great exponent of the art called "logic on fire". And the trouble is that if you think you're there to teach, all you've got is the logic.

That's why I worry when I see that the preacher has come prepared with a PowerPoint presentation. They don't want us to look at them, to share what God has given to them and connect with them through their eyes and their voice: they want us to look at a screen and follow a lecture. That's why I worry about preachers who rely too much on their notes. That's why I worry when preachers are fixated on the Bible, with every statement cross-referenced and every sub-clause analysed. The Word became flesh (John 1:14); we shouldn't turn him back into words.

Preaching comes from the heart and the soul, not just from the mind. Preaching is taking words that are two or three thousand years old, distilling them in the magical retort that is the human mind, and tossing in a lighted match. It's imagination, passion, and conviction. When the preacher stands in the pulpit or at the lectern, the congregation needs to hear not just his or her words, but God himself speaking straight to their hearts and minds.

Do we learn things at the same time? Of course. The preacher will have grappled with the text beforehand, maybe for hours. The commentaries will have been read, the ramifications of different interpretations teased out, the precise sub-species of lion killed by Benaiah the son of Jehoiada in a pit on a snowy day established (1 Chronicles 11:22). Some of this might even find its way into the finished sermon. But that isn't the point of the exercise, any more than building a ski-jump is the point of a different exercise. The point is the opening of the heart and mind to a different reality. A sermon should be dangerous, a whoosh into the unknown with no guarantee of a safe landing.

Teachers and preachers employ some of the same tools. They want to engage the minds of their hearers and help them see things in new ways. The key difference between them is this. The fundamental task of the teacher is to explain. The fundamental task of the preacher is to persuade. The best preachers – even the ones who are popularly known as "teachers" – understand this very well.

They don't just want their hearers to be offered an interesting alternative way of looking at a biblical text or a real-life situation. They are declaring with absolute conviction what they believe is God's truth. And good preachers make us see things their way because they are creative artists, who use words to make us connect ideas and images using the tremendous power of the human imagination – theirs and ours.

Good preachers don't argue that something is true. They show us that it's true, so powerfully that we can't deny it. It's out of these moments of transcendence that conviction comes. Of course we have to go away and test what we've heard. It may be that our conviction lasts no longer than the walk to the car park. But sometimes a meeting with God through an anointed preacher changes us for ever.

There's nothing wrong with teaching – the reverse, in fact. Learning the content of our faith and how to apply it in a complicated, changing world is essential. But I want to argue that preachers should raise their sights. They should take in the Bible study or the home group. Preaching can be different.

So here are some ways of thinking about preaching.

1. It can be like a poem

Not everyone likes poetry. I admit that I live and breathe it. But the key to understanding some poetry, at least, is to realize that the poets are often trying to get you to use your mind in a very particular way. They describe one thing as though it is another thing, and expect you to make the imaginative leap between them.

One of the classic religious poems of the nineteenth century is "Dover Beach", by Matthew Arnold (1822–88). It's actually about the loss of faith; what he sees as its decline, made inevitable by the advances in science and philosophy. It begins with a mesmerizing evocation of the beach at Dover, where "the cliffs of England stand,/ Glimmering and vast, out in the tranquil bay." Then, having set the scene, he continues:

> *The Sea of Faith*
> *Was once, too, at the full, and round earth's shore*
> *Lay like the folds of a bright girdle furled.*
> *But now I only hear*
> *Its melancholy, long, withdrawing roar,*
> *Retreating, to the breath*
> *Of the night-wind, down the vast edges drear*
> *And naked shingles of the world.*

In other words, the retreat of the tide from Dover Beach becomes a metaphor for the retreat of faith from the world.

It's a forceful, convincing use of language, whether you agree with the thinking behind it or not. And, apart from the sheer brilliance of the writing, it's because he has made us use a particular mental muscle: our imagination. He's forced us to make a connection between two different things and create something new.

Sometimes sermons do that. For instance, there's the famous story of Jesus calming the storm, in Matthew 8:23–27. One way of talking about this is to stress the links between the power of Jesus shown in this event and the power of God demonstrated in the Old Testament. The psalmist addresses God, saying: "You rule over the surging sea; when its waves mount up, you still them" (Psalm 89:9); here's Jesus doing the same, an indication of his divinity. For the Hebrews, the sea was a symbol of chaos, like the primeval waters over which the Spirit of God moved in Genesis; so for Jesus to be able to calm it with a word says something about his divine power and relationship to the Father.

Or we could approach it on a purely human level. Jesus was tired and went to sleep, even during a dangerous storm. He had a lot of faith in God, and so should we. These are all good things to say. But what would turn this into a sermon preached instead of just a lesson taught is making the storm stand for something else, as Matthew Arnold did with the receding tide. So the storm is not just wind and water: it's the storms we face in our daily lives. We cope with illness, bereavement, and marital breakdown; with failure, betrayal, and doubt. God seems asleep. He is effectively absent and we struggle alone: but we are never truly abandoned.

And that's when the gospel comes to life in the words of the preacher, because she's made her congregation see the truth in a way that they can't deny.

2. It can be like a drama

One of the greatest television series of recent years, if not the greatest, is the Vince Gilligan creation *Breaking Bad*. It stars Bryan Cranston – previously known as a brilliant comic actor – as Walter White, a chemistry teacher who is told that he has terminal cancer. Desperate to provide for his family and to achieve something in his life, he becomes an expert in the production of crystal meth. The story of his gradual corruption and the terrible effect it has on those around him led no less a figure than Sir Anthony Hopkins to write to Cranston that "what started as a black comedy, descended into a labyrinth of blood, destruction, and hell. It was like a great Jacobean, Shakespearian or Greek tragedy." Hopkins added: "You and all the cast are the best actors I've ever seen."

What *Breaking Bad* does brilliantly is what every other drama tries to do: tell a complicated, sad human story and bring it to an end with a sense of completion. In the final, stunning episode, we feel that the main characters, at least, get what they deserve. That's what the long drama of Scripture does, depicting the great theological arc of paradise lost to paradise regained.

That's what sermons echo. For twenty minutes or half an hour on a Sunday morning, the preacher creates a drama that shows the congregation what their story is and how it ends. He might be retelling an Old Testament tale about prophets or kings. She might be expounding the psalms or a passage from Paul. But at the core of the message we will always be brought to see ourselves, as flawed and sinful yet ultimately redeemed children of God.

When King David had defeated the house of Saul and was safe on his throne, his army was away fighting while David remained at home. He wasn't used to inactivity. He was restless. He saw the wife of one of his soldiers, Uriah the Hittite, bathing on the roof. We know what happened next; she became pregnant and he had Uriah murdered. He was a Middle Eastern king and he could do what he liked: but 2 Samuel 11:27 says, "But the thing David had done displeased the Lord." The next chapter tells of how kings were answerable to prophets. Nathan goes to David and tells him a story. There were two men in a town, one rich and one poor. The rich man had vast flocks and herds; the poor man had one ewe lamb, which he treated as a pet; "it was like a daughter to him". When a traveller comes to town, instead of taking one of his own sheep to feed him, the rich man takes the poor man's lamb.

David is furious: "As surely as the Lord lives, the man who did this must die!" And Nathan, with all a prophet's courage, says to David: "You are the man." Someone else's drama becomes David's drama. Nathan's denunciation and declaration of God's vengeance – "You did it in secret, but I will do this thing in broad daylight before all Israel" – requires a response from him, either rejection or repentance. But it's when he finds his place in Nathan's story that there is the sense of an ending.

3. It can be like a football match

I don't follow the game closely, but I have friends who do. They are exultant on the rare occasions Aston Villa win a game, and in the depths of despair when they lose. A football match – or a tennis match, or any sporting encounter – represents a meeting between teams or individuals who have bent every one of their faculties towards the aim of mastering their opponent. They have trained their bodies to the peak of what they're capable of. They have studied strategy and tactics. If they are remotely serious about what they are doing, they have an intimate knowledge of the rules of the game and how to use them to their advantage. They know how their opponents play and what they'll have to do in order to beat them.

And out of these encounters something extraordinary is created. The crowd is profoundly, sometimes shatteringly, moved by matches played by people they don't know and will never meet. Some of it's because we identify ourselves with the team, so we'll say "we" when we're talking about them, not "they". Some of it's because we admire the skill that they demonstrate. There are moments of beauty when a goal is scored or an unplayable backhand is returned. There's something inspiring about men and women operating at the limits of what the human body can do.

What brings out the best in these people is the element of competition. They test themselves not just against themselves, but against other people. It's in their passionate desire to overcome that they become better than they ever thought they could be. They achieve moments of transcendence and very few of us don't respond to that. Sermons can be like that.

Let's be honest: not every sermon is like a match between Arsenal and Manchester United at Highbury. Some are more like a kick-about in the local park, and that's fair enough. Most of us can't scale Everest-like homiletical heights every Sunday and the gifts of most of us just don't lie in that direction. But most preachers will recognize the feeling of sitting down to prepare their sermon with the light of battle in their eye.

That's because it's hard. The Bible is a difficult book and anyone who says it isn't just hasn't been paying attention. There are layers upon layers of history and theology within its own covers. Then there are the layers of history and theology that make up our own understanding of the Bible. Then there's the need to translate it for today: to bring texts that are two or three thousand years old alive again, in a way that holds people's attention and creates an encounter with the living God.

Sometimes sermons come to preachers and it feels like a gift. We know exactly what the text is saying to us and how we're to convey that to other people. Sometimes – and more often – we struggle. But it's as we wrestle with the hardest opponent of all that our skills develop and our intellectual and spiritual muscles strengthen. It's in the struggle that we find those moments of transcendence. And it's as the congregation recognizes the depth of the preacher's commitment and the costliness of the undertaking that they identify themselves with her and start saying "we".

Towards the end of Genesis 32, Jacob is alone at a ford the night before his fateful meeting with his brother, Esau, whom he's defrauded and betrayed. He has an encounter with a mysterious stranger – call him the Divine – who wrestles with him until daybreak. We're told:

> *When the man saw that he could not overpower*
> *him, he touched the socket of Jacob's hip so that his*
> *hip was wrenched as he wrestled with the man.*
> *Then the man said, "Let me go, for it is daybreak."*
> *But Jacob replied, "I will not let you go unless you*
> *bless me." (25–26)*

Powerful preachers are those who wrestle with God for his blessing. It's the struggle for meaning and the struggle for excellence that create transcendence.

9

Church and state: Why it doesn't always have to be a battle

One day in a Roman marketplace, some time in the second half of the sixth century AD, some merchants were offering their wares for sale. Among the onlookers was a priest named Gregory, who was to become Pope Gregory the Great. Some slave boys were among the merchandise and he noticed their "fair complexions, fine-cut features and beautiful hair". Intrigued, he asked where they were from. "The island of Britain," he was told, "where all the people have this appearance."

"What is the name of this race?" he asked. Told they were Angles, he said: "That is appropriate, for they have angelic faces, and it is right that they should become joint-heirs with the angels in heaven." He asked for the name of the province from which they came; told it was Deira, he answered: "Good. They shall indeed be rescued *de ira* – from wrath – and called to the mercy of Christ."

And, to confirm Gregory's status as the prince of papal

punsters, when he was told the name of their king was Aelle, he replied: "It is right that their land should echo the praise of God our Creator in the word *Alleluia*." Gregory asked the then pope to send him to convert the Angles. Nothing came of that, but when he became pope himself he sent Augustine, who in 597 became the first Archbishop of Canterbury.

He wasn't the first Christian in Britain by any means. Christianity had appeared with the Romans and there was a native British or Celtic church that survived the onslaught of the pagans after the eclipse of Rome. But the church's reach and power grew as the Anglo-Saxons were converted and came to dominate what became England. The church's organization survived the collapse of Rome. It had scholars and administrators. It knew how to do things. It became indispensable to government. The state needed it.

In round numbers, and give or take a century or so, Britain has been a Christian country for nearly 1,500 years. Our laws have been based on principles of justice derived originally from the ancient customs of the various tribes who invaded us, but also from the Bible. We have been taught, Sunday by Sunday for a millennium and a half, to think of right and wrong within a framework that has been thoroughly and exclusively Christian.

That's not to say that the law has always reflected the highest Christian ideals – far from it. As Byron wrote in his mock-epic poem *Don Juan*, "Christians have burned each other, quite persuaded/ That all the Apostles would have done as they did." But the terms of the debate were Christian. The underlying question was, "What is right in the eyes of God?" The theological shorthand for that kind of society is *Christendom*. And Christendom is crumbling.

This isn't the place for a cultural history of the last hundred years. Let's just acknowledge what we all know: that during the lifetime of people who are reading this book in middle age, everything has changed. Attitudes towards moral and ethical questions aren't formed with reference to what we think God might approve of. They're formed by what people believe – rightly or wrongly – is the kindest or fairest thing to do, or what gives people the maximum freedom to choose. Arguments about right and wrong in the abstract gain no traction at all.

This means in practice that there are collisions between what are called "traditional values" and the demands of the law, which has developed in a way that aims to protect the interests of people who've sometimes suffered very considerably because of those values. In the UK, this law is expressed in the 2010 Equality Act. You cannot discriminate against someone in access to education or employment or in the provision of goods or services. If they can show they've suffered worse treatment because of a "protected characteristic" – because they're disabled, transgender, of a minority race, or because of their religion or belief, their gender, or their sexual orientation – the law has been broken.

Look at the way people have been treated in the past because of all these characteristics. Generally speaking, we know better now. But if the world's a better place for women teachers, for instance, who used to have to give up their jobs if they married (a senior judge said in 1925: "The duty of a married woman is primarily to look after her domestic concerns and it is impossible for her to do so and to effectively and satisfactorily act as a teacher at the same time") it's because the law was changed. If it's a better place for someone who could have been denied work because his skin is black, it's because the law was changed. If someone who's homosexually orientated no longer has to fear arrest and imprisonment, it's because the law was changed.

In each of these cases there was landmark legislation – in 1944, 1965, and 1967 respectively – that laid the foundations for further reforms over several decades. For many people, the Equality Act was the culmination of that work: its effect was to say, "We won't allow you to be held back because of things about you that you can't control."

It's brilliant. It's not perfect, but it helps make Britain a better place. And yet, and yet. What happens when a Christian registrar decides that she cannot in all conscience conduct same-sex weddings? In January 2013, Lillian Ladele lost her case at the European Court of Human Rights. She was a registrar in Islington and had claimed she had suffered religious discrimination because she refused to officiate at same-sex weddings; the court disagreed.

What happens when Christian guest-house owners feel they can't let people of the same gender share a double room? In November 2013 Peter and Hazelmary Bull, who in 2008 had refused to let gay couple Steven Preddy and Martyn Hall share a room, finally had their case rejected by the Supreme Court.

What happens when a Christian-run bakery declines to bake a cake for a gay customer because he asked them to put a slogan on it in support of gay marriage? In May 2015, Ashers Bakery found out: a Belfast court found it guilty of discrimination.

These are British examples. There are plenty from the US, too. Take Kim Davis, the county clerk in Kentucky who became a talking point in 2015 when she refused to issue marriage licences to same-sex couples. She went to jail rather than do it, and won high-profile support from politicians such as

Mike Huckabee, a candidate for the Republican presidential nomination, who said that her imprisonment was part of a move towards the "criminalization of Christianity".

What happens when anti-discrimination laws are felt to discriminate against people who believe they're upholding a view that's good, right, and true? Is there a conspiracy against Christianity? Are we in a culture war that could see the end of 1,500 years of history unless we fight tooth and nail to preserve it?

The short answer is, no. But there's a temptation to believe that when Christians are stopped from doing something that they've always thought they had a right to do, it's an attack on our faith. We tend to react with opposition. What's actually happening is that, instead of dictating what happens, we're in a marketplace of ideas. To be taken seriously, we have to be able to argue not just that something is right in absolute terms, but that it contributes to the overall well-being of a society in which practising, churchgoing Christians are in a considerable minority.

That's not to say that our 1,500 years of history can simply be undone. In April 2014 David Cameron declared that the UK is still a "Christian country". He was backed by the Archbishop of Canterbury, Justin Welby, who said: "It is a historical fact (perhaps unwelcome to some, but true) that our main systems of ethics, the way we do law and justice, the values of society, how we decide what is fair, the protection of the poor, and most of the way we look at society... All have been shaped by and founded on Christianity." It's fair to say that Mr Cameron's comments touched off something of a firestorm. Many said that his remarks were divisive. But, at a historical and social level, as the Archbishop said, he was right.

We're now in a situation in which Christians no longer control the agenda. But does this mean that our reaction should be to regret what has passed and fight a desperate rearguard action to reclaim it? Should we resist change by lobbying politicians, using the courts, passive resistance, and fervent prayers for national righteousness? Does everything have to be a battle, or is there a better way?

In my work as a journalist I'm exposed to the best of Christianity. I read countless stories of people behaving with kindness, decency, and self-sacrificial love. I'm exposed to other things, too. Many Christians feel passionately about particular causes. That passion leads them to denigrate those who don't agree with them, or who don't feel the same. It leads them to make claims about the place of Christians and Christianity that aren't true and can't be justified. It helps to build a sense that Christians are embattled, a tiny minority of righteous people faced with the might of an oppressive, aggressively secularizing state.

The Archbishop of York, John Sentamu, gave a great answer to this in an interview with *The Spectator* in January 2015. He was speaking on the publication of a collection of essays entitled *On Rock or Sand? Firm Foundations for Britain's Future.* Asked whether he thought Christians in the UK were being persecuted, he said: "I lived in Uganda during the time of Idi Amin… and our archbishop was murdered by Idi Amin. I had to get out of Uganda because I had opposed Amin on a number of things which I didn't think were ethically right… I know what persecution looks like. What is happening at the moment in England, it ain't persecution."

When Christians are too quick to cry persecution, we lose credibility. Worse, we come across as clinging fiercely to our right to discriminate and to treat people worse than the rest of society does. As I write, a pastor in Northern Ireland, James McConnell, has been found not guilty in a Belfast court on charges related to a sermon he preached. In it he called Islam a satanic religion. "Islam is heathen, Islam is satanic, Islam is a doctrine spawned in hell," he said. He likened Muslims to the IRA, saying there were cells spread right across the UK. He also said: "Now people say there are good Muslims in Britain – that may be so – but I don't trust them."

The problem was that the sermon was broadcast over the internet, which meant that he fell foul of the Communications Act. McConnell was charged with "improper use of a public electronic communications network and causing a grossly offensive message to be sent by means of a public electronic communications network". He was backed not only by evangelical Christians – who turned out in their hundreds to show their support during his court appearances and made the case a subject of prayer across the province – but by Muslims and atheists too. They argued that the key issue was one of freedom of speech. Just because someone says something that you don't like, it doesn't mean that the law should stop them. No one has a right not to be offended.

For the record, I'm glad the judge decided the case as he did. I want people to have the freedom to say what they believe. I think if you make things unsayable in public where everyone can hear them, people will say them in private where no one's going to call them out on how wrong they are. But I'm sad that, alongside their jubilation at the result, there weren't more Christians prepared to say, "Oh, and by the way: you don't talk about people like that. It isn't Christlike and it isn't right."

If we use our freedom to abuse people and discriminate against them, we're misusing it. The apostle Paul says in

Galatians 5:13: "You, my brothers and sisters, were called to be free. But do not use your freedom to indulge the flesh; rather, serve one another humbly in love." When he says "flesh", he doesn't mean our physical bodies. He means the part of our nature that is orientated away from God. The context is different – Paul is talking about how Christians should behave towards each other, not how they should behave towards wider society – but the seed of the idea is there. Christians are called to a different way of living entirely. We aren't called to assert our own rights, but to be the servants of others.

Does this mean that we should just accept whatever changes our wider society decides to enact or assume, without offering an alternative? Absolutely not. In the Bible, there are two competing views of the state. One is that it's beneficial; it's instituted by God, and we should be grateful for it. The other is that it's at best a concession to human weakness and at worst demonic and oppressive.

In the Old Testament, we can see this reflected in the way the prophet Samuel responds to the request of the people of Israel for a king. The story is told in 1 Samuel 8. Samuel is old, and it's obvious to the elders of Israel that his sons are not the men their father was. So they ask for a king to lead them, as the other nations have. God tells Samuel to warn them about what their king will do. He'll make their sons serve in his army and their daughters serve in his household. "He will take a tenth of your flocks, and you yourselves will become his slaves. When that day comes, you will cry out for relief from the king you have chosen, but the Lord will not answer you in that day" (17–18). Samuel does not approve of their choice, and many of the kings of Israel and Judah proved him right. But some of them were men who did right and walked closely with God, and God blessed them.

The New Testament shows the same tension. In Romans 13 Paul says: "Let everyone be subject to the governing authorities, for there is no authority except that which God has established. The authorities that exist have been established by God. Consequently, whoever rebels against them is rebelling against what God has instituted, and those who do so will bring judgment on themselves. For rulers hold no terror for those who do right, but for those who do wrong" (1–3).

That's clear enough; but in the book of Revelation, the picture of the state is very different. In Revelation – written against the background of Nero's persecution, when the streets of Rome were lit by the bodies of Christians being burned alive for their faith – the state is a ravening beast. It's a dragon; it is "Babylon the great, the mother of prostitutes and of the abominations of the earth" (17:5).

States are instituted by God. States are Babylon. These truths are in an eternal tension. What it means for Christians is that we're in tension too. We don't blindly go along with everything the state demands. When we do that, we can end up complicit in terrible evil.

In my own Baptist tradition, when the 1934 Baptist World Congress was held in Nazi Berlin a huge swastika was displayed beside a painting of the crucifixion. Three years later, when an international ecumenical conference criticized Hitler's treatment of the Jews and expressed support for the Confessing Church (with which Dietrich Bonhoeffer was associated), the Baptist and Methodist delegates publicly protested. They said that Hitler had left them free to preach and evangelize, and that was what really mattered. One Baptist writer said: "National Socialism has kindly let us do as we like because we stay away from politics."

Sometimes it ought to be obvious that the state is Babylon. Mostly, it's more complicated. Some things the state allows or promotes, most Christians will agree with. They fit our personal and corporate ideas of what's right. For instance, we believe it's right to help people who are poor or ill, so we approve of social security and a good national health service. We believe in education, so we approve of schools and colleges and universities.

What happens when the state does something we don't approve of? Sometimes there'll be matters on which the issues are absolutely clear. At these times the church can speak with one voice. If this country made it legal to torture people, or to persecute them because of their political opinions, or if it launched a war of aggression, we would all say "No" (though it's worth saying that in previous centuries none of this behaviour would have been seriously questioned; the thing was to make sure you were persecuting the right people).

Mostly, though, the causes that exercise Christian pressure groups whose press releases arrive in my inbox aren't as clear-cut. There's no doubt that some battles need to be fought. A parliamentary perennial is the attempt to legalize "assisted dying", for instance. When someone decides that their life has become not worth living, the argument runs, they should be helped to end it. In the abstract, I don't have a problem with that. In practice, I have severe misgivings. My instinct is that it would inevitably expose vulnerable people to appalling moral pressure to end things early. I think even when people believe they have the purest motives imaginable – the relief of other people's suffering – they're likely to be influenced by a much less worthy desire: the relief of their own discomfort at the sight of it.

I suspect that in spite of the opposition of many people – of all religions and none –some form of assisted dying will become legal in my lifetime. But what our testimonies and protests can do is modify, shape, and inform that legislation. People who believe as I do won't like it. But our voices will have been heard, and if an act legalizing assisted dying is passed, it will be better than it would have been if we'd said nothing. It will have been said, loudly and clearly, that people are not disposable; that from their first breath to their last, they are free and precious individuals whose lives are to be cherished.

This is one example of what engagement with our wider culture can do. We've helped to shape the debate. Another is over same-sex marriage and how the right of gay people not to suffer discrimination plays out against the right to hold, and to manifest, sincere religious beliefs. There are immensely complicated legal issues surrounding these questions (anything that requires the European Court of Human Rights to adjudicate is not going to be straightforward). Dealing with them properly would double the length of this book, but let's say this: we're in a position where there are competing rights that are not always reconcilable.

It isn't always going to be possible for a conservative Christian to express what they feel about gay marriage, either in words or by their actions. That is not necessarily the state behaving like Babylon. It might be the state trying, as carefully as it can, to treat everyone as fairly as possible.

Of course, there need to be safeguards. If a church decides it doesn't want to perform same-sex marriages, it shouldn't have to; and because of the conversations that the churches have had, they won't be forced into that position. Whether it's over same-sex marriage or anything else, Christian churches – and other faiths – need to be given the maximum possible freedom that's achievable in a society where everyone has rights.

And I'm glad that other people have rights. I don't want to live in a society that tries to impose godliness by law. That's what started to happen when Christianity became dominant in the Roman Empire under Constantine (306–37). Under Emperor Theodosius, in 380, Christianity was proclaimed as the official and only religion of the Empire. From then on the church, hand in glove with the state, imposed faith rather than offered it – and punished departures from it, sometimes with extreme brutality. Even the great Reformers of the sixteenth and seventeenth centuries thought you could do that.

Of course, you can't. Faith is personal, or it's nothing at all. I believe we should seek to protect our freedom to believe and to practise our faith, and that we should seek that for others too. But I also believe Christians shouldn't be afraid of powerlessness. We should even rejoice in it, because we aren't called to power but to surrender.

For many Christians this goes against the grain. It's because of something called the Elijah Syndrome. Elijah was one of the greatest of the Old Testament prophets. He lived in the wilderness (1 Kings 17:6), where the ravens fed him on bread and meat (probably carrion). He stood up against King Ahab when it was dangerous to do so. He stood alone against the prophets of Baal on Mount Carmel, and prevailed (1 Kings 18). He fled to Mount Horeb, where he told God: "The Israelites have rejected your covenant, torn down your altars, and put your prophets to death with the sword. I am the only one left, and now they are trying to kill me too" (19:10).

The idea of being like Elijah is very attractive. The notion that everyone else has fallen away and that we're part of a small but pure group, the only ones left keeping the faith, is quite seductive. Condemning those who don't agree with us, or who don't speak the same theological language, is the way the Elijah complex shows itself.

There are times when God anoints an Elijah, but it doesn't happen very often. We need to be very wary of talking up the church's "prophetic" role. It usually means denouncing someone or something, and that isn't always very helpful. More appropriate for our thinking about how Christians relate to the wider world are the similes Jesus himself offered.

He said: "You are the salt of the earth" (Matthew 5:13).

He said: "You are the light of the world" (Matthew 5:14).

He said: "The kingdom of heaven is like yeast" (Matthew 13:33).

These aren't images that speak of domination. They speak of transformation. The question of same-sex relationships is an evangelical pressure point. Some find they can accept their validity from a theological point of view; most can't. But, for those who can't, here's a way of looking at it that I think is true to what Jesus said.

I think the law forbidding discrimination is, in principle, correct. I think it represents a moral advance. I don't believe you should be able to refuse to serve someone just because they're gay and you're not – or vice versa. And I really do know and understand what that means for people who believe that their sincere, deep and perhaps costly views about sexuality mean that they can't comply. I can see what it means for the bed-and-breakfast owner who feels profoundly that hosting a gay couple would mean condoning sin. I think they're wrong – I think that someone's personal moral decisions are virtually irrelevant beside the huge question of whether they know Christ as their saviour – but I understand.

But here's the other thing: I can see what it means for that gay couple who are turned away at the door, too. I can imagine the hurt, the perceived insult, and the anger. When these deeply held beliefs are seen as competing, there are going to be winners and losers – and because the social current is running in a particular direction, it is going to be conservative Christians who are the losers. I'm not happy about that. I do worry about a moral uniformity being imposed on us that leaves less and less space for dissenters. But neither am I happy with the image of the Christian as the person who is always saying "No", resisting change to the last ditch, convinced that he or she is the world's victim.

So how about this: what happens if Christians resolve not to play the world's game at all? What happens if we don't stand on our rights and if we don't feel that we have to adjudicate other people's moral decisions? What happens if, instead of trying as hard as we can to win our case, we try as hard as we can to show grace? Because one of the problems with court cases is that both sides lose, no matter who wins. Both of them look self-righteous, vindictive, and petty.

One of the things that Jesus did with divine effectiveness was to subvert the legalistic, honour–shame conventions of his day. In Matthew 5:38–41 he tells someone who has been struck on the right cheek – a Roman's insulting backhander – to offer the left: "I'm a man like you, so hit me like a man." A grasping creditor is shamed because he doesn't even leave his debtor with a coat to keep himself warm. A Roman legionary who press-gangs a Jew to carry a load for a legal mile ends up in a world of trouble because the obliging victim insists on carrying it for two. He goes on: "Love your enemies, and pray for those who persecute you."

People who don't believe the same things that we do aren't our enemies, but all too often we act as if they are. Sometimes people say, "Just because you're a Christian it doesn't mean you should just stand there and take it when people attack you." It's usually an encouragement to stand up and fight – and often about the wrong thing. Actually, though, it's right. You don't just stand there and take it. You step forward, and embrace.

Imagine this: instead of standing up for their rights, going to court, and providing the media with great stories about discrimination against Christians – or Christians discriminating against other people – Christians who believe that homosexual relations are profoundly wrong decide to do something completely different.

They realize that their disapproval probably isn't going to make anyone agree with them. It won't make anyone act any differently, and, if it did, so what? They still wouldn't know Jesus. All they would know is that Christians are people who reject them. So these conservative Christians decide that they'll bake that cake or offer that hotel room or officiate at that wedding, and do it gladly – and leave the outcome to God.

Instead of being Elijah, they're being salt, light, and yeast. That, after all, is what Jesus told us to do.

THE PRODIGAL EVANGELICAL

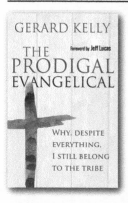

WHY, DESPITE EVERYTHING, I STILL BELONG TO THE TRIBE

"In this beautiful book, I hear the sounds of dancing and music. Gerard's winsome, authentic, and hope-laden words will warm the coldest heart, and bring us back to this core truth: the good news really is very, very good. Highly recommended."

– Jeff Lucas

The Christian faith is about grace, not law, yet evangelicals so often get it wrong. Gerard uses the story of the Prodigal Son to unpack this vital idea and to explain why he is still willing to be called an evangelical – because the Christian story centres on the breadth and depth of God's love. This is the narrative at the heart of the faith. We can't afford to lose it.

"Does what all good books do – it engages my heart, captures my imagination, challenges my assumptions, and stretches my thinking. I am privileged to call this man my friend."

– Malcolm Duncan

"What a fantastic book – destined to be a classic of Christian literature."

– Bev Murrill

"Biblical, theological, culturally perceptive, and above all disarmingly honest. A must read for anyone wondering if 'evangelical' is a word worth saving!"

– Anna Norman Walker

ISBN: 978-0-85721-626-7 | e-ISBN: 978-0-85721-627-4

THE INTROVERT CHARISMATIC

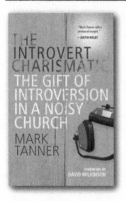

THE GIFT OF INTROVERSION IN A NOISY CHURCH

"Mark Tanner offers profound insight."

— JUSTIN WELBY

Extrovert characters, exuberant worship, large crowds and noisy fellowship seem central to charismatic churches – but do we really need to shout before God will move in power?

Introverts can find charismatic culture off-putting, even disagreeable, and yet love what God is doing. How can they engage in a healthy manner? Is introversion something to be overcome, grown out of, even healed?

"It is none of those things," emphasizes Mark Tanner. "Introversion is a creation gift. It is part of the image of God." He explores the richness of worshipping God with the personality you have been given. The Church, the Kingdom, and the world need charismatic introverts and this book is a thoughtful and practical guide for introverts and extroverts alike.

ISBN: 978-0-85721-588-8 | e-ISBN: 978-0-85721-589-5

GAGGING JESUS

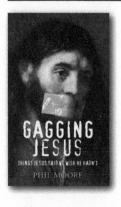

Things Jesus Said We Wish He Hadn't

"Whether you are a believer or merely a curious sceptic, this book will help you to discover Jesus as he really is."

— **Sandy Millar, co-founder of the Alpha Course**

Jesus of Nazareth wasn't afraid to tell it like it is. Those who claim to follow him, on the other hand, often are.

It's easy to settle for a tamed and domesticated Jesus. A bound-and-gagged Jesus. A Jesus of our own thinking. That's why this book focuses on the fifteen most outrageous things Jesus said: the fifteen things you are least likely to hear preached about in church.

If you ever suspected that Jesus wasn't crucified for acting like a polite vicar in a pair of socks and sandals, then this book is for you. Fasten your seatbelt and get ready to discover the real Jesus in all his outrageous, ungagged glory.

"Downright dangerous! It demands attention. Prepare to be shocked, undone, and put back together again."
— **Greg Haslam, Senior Pastor, Westminster Chapel, London, UK**

ISBN: 978-0-85721-453-9 | e-ISBN: 978-0-85721-454-6

The Atheist Who Didn't Exist

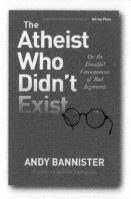

*Or: the Dreadful Consequences
of Bad Arguments*

"A positive whoosh of fresh air."
– Adrian Plass

"Intelligent, funny and elegant."
– Michael Coren

In the last decade, atheism has leapt from obscurity to the front pages: producing best-selling books, making movies, and plastering adverts on the side of buses. There's an energy and a confidence to contemporary atheism: many people now assume that a godless scepticism is the default position, indeed the only position for anybody wishing to appear educated, contemporary, and urbane. Atheism is hip, religion is boring.

Yet when one pokes at popular atheism, many of the arguments used to prop it up quickly unravel. The Atheist Who Didn't Exist is designed to expose some of the loose threads on the cardigan of atheism, tug a little, and see what happens. Blending humour with serious thought, Andy Bannister helps the reader question everything, assume nothing and, above all, recognise lazy scepticism and bad arguments. Be an atheist by all means: but do be a thought-through one.

ISBN: 978-0-85721-610-6 | e-ISBN: 978-0-85721-611-3